PUB WALKS IN DORSET

Anne-Marie Edwards

COUNTRYSIDE BOOKS
NEWBURY BERKSHIRE

First published 2013
© Anne-Marie Edwards 2013
Updated and reprinted 2021, 2025

All rights reserved. No reproduction permitted without the prior permission of the publisher:

COUNTRYSIDE BOOKS
3 Catherine Road
Newbury, Berkshire

To view our complete range of books, please visit us at
www.countrysidebooks.co.uk

ISBN 978 1 84674 282 8

All materials used in the manufacture of this book carry FSC certification

Designed by Peter Davies, Nautilus Design
Produced through MRM Associated Ltd, Tadley
Printed by The Holywell Press, Oxford

Contents

	Area map	4
	Introduction	6
	Acknowledgements	7

WALK

1	**Kingston:** The Scott Arms *(3½ miles)*	8
2	**Corfe Castle:** The Greyhound Inn *(4½ miles)*	13
3	**Lytchett Minster:** St Peters Finger *(4½ miles)*	18
4	**Corfe Mullen (Lambs Green):** The Lambs Green Inn *(3 miles)*	22
5	**Horton:** The Horton Inn *(5¼ miles)*	27
6	**Iwerne Courtney:** The Cricketers *(2½ miles)*	32
7	**Tarrant Gunville:** Home Farm *(4½ miles)*	37
8	**Tarrant Keyneston:** The True Lovers Knot *(4 miles)*	41
9	**Winterborne Zelston:** The Botany Bay Inne *(4 miles)*	46
10	**Moreton:** The Frampton Arms *(3 miles)*	50
11	**Winterborne Stickland:** The Crown Inn *(4½ miles)*	55
12	**Shillingstone:** The Old Ox Inn *(5 or 4 miles)*	59
13	**Hinton St Mary:** The White Horse Inn *(5½ miles)*	63

Area Map Showing Locations of the Walks

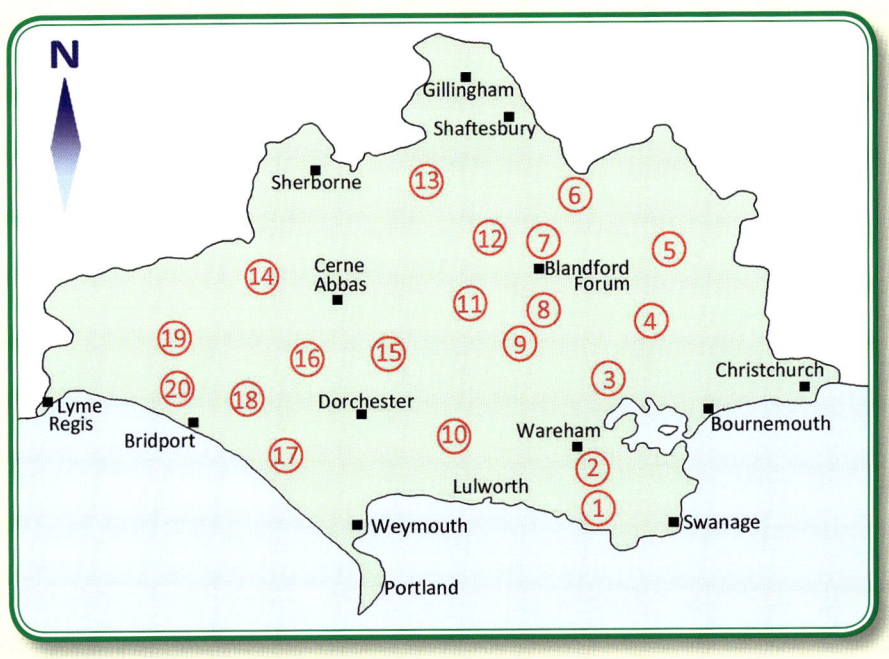

WALK

14	**Evershot:** The Acorn Inn *(4 miles)*	68
15	**Cerne Abbas:** The New Inn *(2¾ miles)*	72
16	**Cattistock:** The Fox and Hounds *(4½ miles)*	76
17	**Abbotsbury:** The Swan Inn *(4 miles)*	81
18	**Loders:** The Loders Arms *(4½ miles)*	85
19	**Stoke Abbott:** The New Inn *(4½ miles)*	89
20	**Eype:** Eype's Mouth Country Hotel *(2½ miles)*	93

PUBLISHER'S NOTE

We hope that you obtain considerable enjoyment from this book; great care has been taken in its preparation. However, changes of landlord and actual closures are sadly not uncommon. Likewise, although at the time of publication all routes followed public rights of way or permitted paths, diversion orders can be made and permissions withdrawn.

We cannot, of course, be held responsible for such diversion orders and any inaccuracies in the text which result from these or any other changes to the routes, nor any damage which might result from walkers trespassing on private property. We are anxious though that all details covering the walks and the pubs are kept up to date and would therefore welcome information from readers which would be relevant to future editions.

The simple sketch maps that accompany the walks in the book are based on notes made by the author whilst checking out the routes on the ground. For the benefit of a proper map, however, we do recommend that you purchase the relevant Ordnance Survey sheet covering your walk. The Ordnance Survey maps are widely available, especially through booksellers and local newsagents.

INTRODUCTION

I have written several books about Dorset and the more I explore this magical county the more I find to charm and delight me. The aim of this book is to share this enchantment with you. Dorset is rural England at its most tranquil and unhurried. The countryside is outstandingly beautiful and, although Dorset is a small county, once you leave the busy roads you will discover an amazing variety of scenery. It is said that after a tour in Dorset you will have seen three-quarters of England!

For this book I have chosen some of my family's favourite walks. These include a ramble along Dorset's magnificent Jurassic coast near Eype, leisurely strolls in the southern uplands of Cranborne Chase, once a great hunting forest and still famous for its ancient beech woods, and walks in the Blackmore Vale, a small world of high-hedged lanes and flower-filled meadows. Hidden in deep valleys carved by chalk streams, you will discover some of Dorset's most charming villages. They are as varied as the scenery. Many roofs are dark-thatched. Walls can be built of whatever materials came to hand from humble cob to glowing honey-coloured stone from Ham Hill. In the Purbeck Hills, whole villages are built and roofed with stone from local quarries.

All the walks start at or close to an excellent pub where you can be assured of a warm welcome and good food and drink. Opening hours and meal times were accurate when I called but these can vary. It is a good idea to telephone or consult the pub's website to confirm before your visit. The publicans I spoke to were happy to allow patrons to leave cars while they walk but they do ask us to have a word with them first.

The routes are circular and between 2½ and 5¾ miles in length. Each walk is accompanied by a simple sketch map designed to guide you to the starting point and give an overall picture of the route. But for all the extra information you may need I recommend you arm yourself with the relevant Ordnance Survey Explorer or Outdoor Leisure map noted in the introduction to each walk.

The Dorset countryside can be muddy even after light rainfall so it is best to wear boots or strong shoes, especially on the coast path where extra grip is always needed. It is usually wise to carry a waterproof with a hood and I think it is a good idea to defeat attacks by nettles by wearing long trousers not shorts. Finally I wish you many happy and rewarding hours on foot in Dorset.

Anne-Marie Edwards

ACKNOWLEDGEMENTS

As always when I write about Dorset I am most grateful to Edward and Marie Swann who helped me with the research and shared with me their love of Dorset. My thanks also to Deidre Sprackling in Winterborne Stickland post office for information about the Hambro family, Denise Rose who gave me valuable information about Lytchett Minster and to Captain Dick Snell for the cover picture. I would also like to thank Paula Leigh and all my friends at Countryside Books for helping to make writing this book such a pleasure. Finally, I must thank the members of my team, our daughter Julie whose enthusiasm and cheerful support never fails, and my husband Mike, my companion on every step of the way.

POOH STICKS BRIDGE IN WINTERBORNE ZELSTON

Kingston
The Scott Arms
3½ miles (5.6 km)

The Dorset Coast is famous for its spectacular scenery. This walk takes you to the sea along the crest of a high downland ridge with splendid views over one of Dorset's loveliest valleys, known as the Golden Bowl. The route leads to Houns-tout, a dramatic cliff-top overlooking Chapman's Pool, an incredibly blue, scallop-shaped bay.

The walk starts in Kingston, an attractive village built and roofed with the local dove-grey limestone standing high in the Purbeck Hills. A woodland path leads to open downland. On your right the hillsides drop smooth and sheer to the wooded banks of a stream flowing through the Golden Bowl. At the seaward end you will see 18th-century Encombe House. After following the down to Houns-tout and enjoying wonderful views over the Dorset coast, you take a valley path to return to Kingston.

Kingston – *The Scott Arms*

The **SCOTT ARMS** is a splendid pub offering a warm welcome and excellent food and drink. There are plenty of quiet corners but the main bar area is light and roomy with high ceilings, white-washed stone walls and polished pine. Real ales include a range from local breweries, as well as guest ales. Ciders include traditional scrumpy on draught and there is an extensive wine list. Seasonal menus are sourced as far as possible from Purbeck suppliers offering an exciting choice of meals. You can enjoy game dishes in winter, fresh seafood in summer and delicious locally-grown vegetables.

From the garden there is a breathtaking view over Corfe Castle framed in the hills. In the far distance there is a glimpse of Poole harbour. A mounted telescope has become a permanent fixture!

Bed and Breakfast is available.

✆ 01929 480270; postcode BH20 5LH

How to get there: Drive through Corfe, heading south on the A351. Turn right for Kingston along the B3069. At the top of the hill, turn right past the front of the Scott Arms, then turn right again into the pub car park.
Parking: The Scott Arms car park.
Map: OS Explorer Outdoor Leisure 15 Purbeck and South Dorset (GR: SY958797).

THE WALK

1 Turn right from the entrance to the Scott Arms and walk up the stone-flagged pavement beside the main street of the village and follow the sign for Encombe. You pass St James' church on your left. The church seems far too big for such a small village particularly as there is another church (now a private house) in Kingston. St James' was completed in 1880 as a private chapel for the third Earl of Eldon, owner of the Encombe Estate which includes Kingston. The interior is magnificent, with Purbeck marble columns and fine wrought-iron work.

Keep straight on past a turning on the right and the drive to Kingston House and follow the track bearing a little left, signed 'Hounstout'. This brings you to another footpath signed 'Hounstout' which leads uphill through the woods of Kingston Plantation.

Pub Walks in Dorset

2 You leave the trees to enjoy your first view of the Golden Bowl and Encombe House, a fine building faced with white ashlar and decorated with porticoes and columns.

In 1807 the Encombe Estate was bought by the Lord Chancellor, John Scott, who took the title Earl of Eldon. John Scott's life reads like a fairy tale. A poor boy born in Love Lane in Newcastle, he fell in love with a rich banker's daughter, Bessie Surtees. The parents of both objected to their marriage so he kidnapped Bessie and married her. He made a fortune and remained devoted to Bessie all his life. He erected the obelisk you will see on the opposite hilltop in 1835, in memory of his brother who became Lord Stowell.

Follow the path over stiles along the crest of the ridge to the cliff-top at Houns-tout to meet the Dorset Coast Path.

3 Bear left along the cliff-top path as it curves round the edge of Houns-tout. Looking ahead you will see St Aldhelm's Head crowned with the tiny Norman chapel dedicated to St Aldhelm, the 8th-century Bishop of Sherborne. I came this way in late July and clumps of nettles either side of the path attracted swarms of butterflies including red admirals, peacocks and small tortoiseshells. The path curves a little left and below you lies a perfectly rounded cove, Chapman's Pool. The surrounding cliffs crumble easily, resulting in landslips. When smuggling luxury goods from France was rife along the south coast, it is said that some coastguards, with eyes on their safety, asked smugglers not to land their contraband there!

4 Descend the stone-edged steps with care to the foot of the hill.

5 Turn left over a stile and keep ahead following the sign 'Coast Path to Hill Bottom ¾'. Continue up this strangely remote valley. The path curves right through a gate to meet a lane. Turn left and follow the lane which runs gently uphill and becomes metalled as it passes the trees of Kingston Plantation. The road follows South Street, passing St James' church on the left, to descend into Kingston. Turn right and walk down the village street to return to the Scott Arms and your car.

Kingston – The Scott Arms

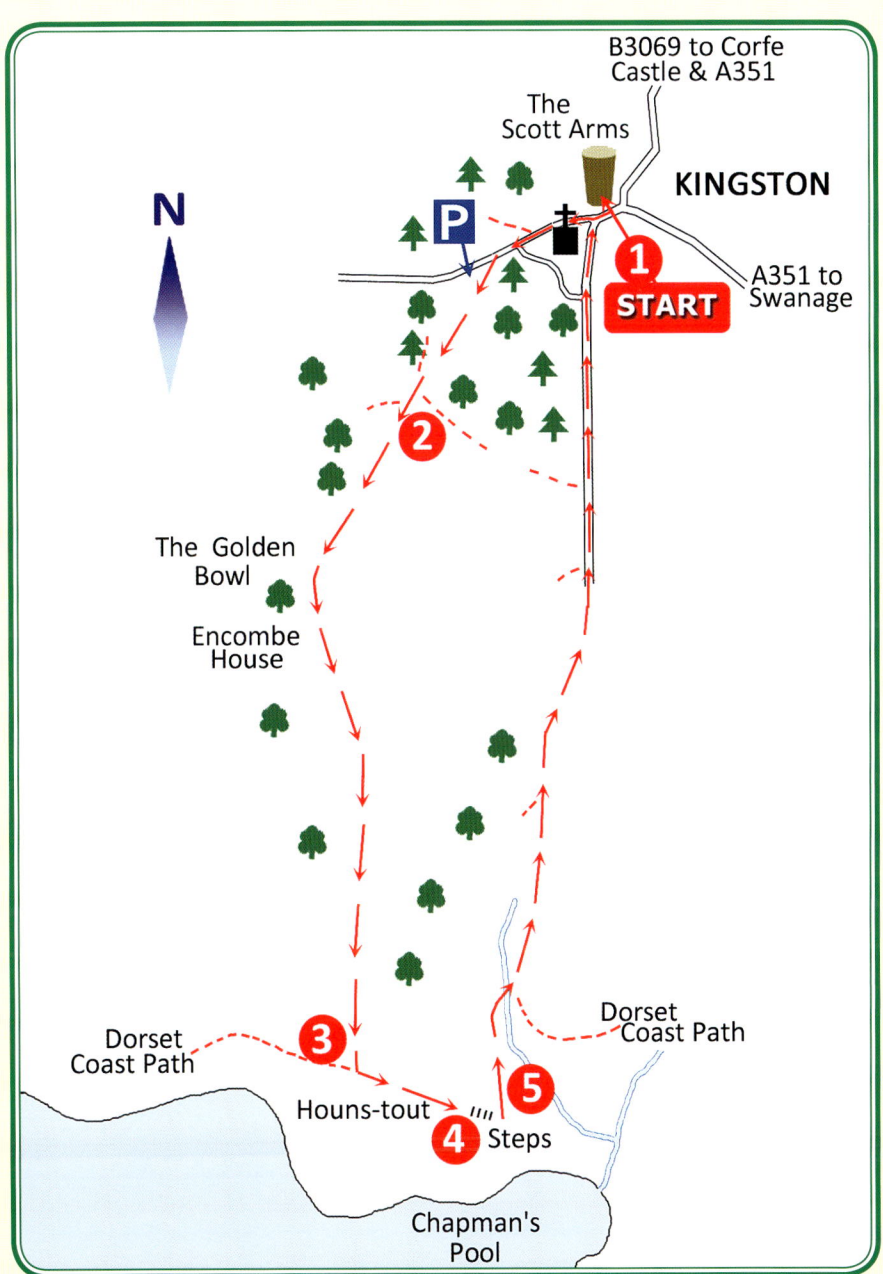

Pub Walks in Dorset

> ### PLACE OF INTEREST NEARBY
>
> **The Purbeck Stone Museum** is an excellent museum in Langton Matravers, 3 miles east of Kingston, beside the B3069. Stone has been quarried on the Isle of Purbeck for over 2,000 years. The topmost layer can be polished to resemble marble and reveal glowing colours of blue-grey, green and red, making it eminently suitable for church building and decoration. Purbeck limestone was quarried and exported to London to rebuild the city after the Great Fire. The museum tells the story of the stone industry and depicts the working life of a stonemason. It is open from 1st April to 30th September.
> ✆ 01929 423168; postcode BH19 3HZ

THE STEPS ON THE WAY TO CHAPMAN'S POOL

CORFE CASTLE
The Greyhound Inn
4½ miles (7.2 km)

Corfe Castle stands high, guarding a pass in a glorious range of downland running from Lulworth Cove in the west to Ballard Point overlooking Swanage Bay in the east. The castle gives its name to the village at its foot. It is a wonderful area for walks and this downland stroll is one of the most enjoyable, giving panoramic views.

The walk starts at the approach to Corfe Castle village. A wide grassy path leads you gradually up the side of Rollington Hill. You follow the crest of the down to Brenscombe Hill before descending to a quiet valley road at Woolgarston. After taking a footpath to Little Woolgarston, a path through Corfe Common Nature Reserve brings you to the Square in Corfe Castle village and the Greyhound Inn. You return to your car along a path below the castle ramparts.

Pub Walks in Dorset

The **GREYHOUND INN** is a venerable coaching inn and one of the oldest in England. Originally the building was divided into three cottages, parts of which date from 1580. In front of the entrance three sturdy pillars support an upper room which overhangs the pavement. Inside you feel little has changed since the inn's coaching days. Below the heavily beamed ceilings, tables are tucked away into alcoves beside deep-set windows. There is a wide range of beverages on offer with cask ales and ciders sourced from local breweries like The Dorset Brewing Company, Ringwood Brewery and the Purbeck Cider Company. The menu offers a wide selection of locally sourced ingredients which include vegan and gluten free options. Smaller dishes and larger plates are both available along with a delicious list of desserts.
☏ 01929 480205; postcode BH20 5EZ

> **How to get there:** Follow the A351 towards Corfe Castle. Pass the National Trust Corfe Castle car park and information centre on your left, turn right along the road signed for Church Knowle, Steeple and Kimmeridge and park immediately on your right.
> **Parking:** As detailed above.
> **Map:** OS Outdoor Leisure 15 Purbeck and South Dorset (GR: SY959825).

THE WALK

1. Return to the main road and turn right along the pavement with the castle mound on your right. When the road rises, cross over, and turn left up Sandy Hill Lane to go under a railway bridge. Continue up the lane past a footpath on your left.

2. Just past a parking area turn left through a gate and follow the bridleway leading up the down. As you gain height, look back for a splendid view of the castle and the western downs.

3. The path divides by one of the marker stones you will see along this route. Keep ahead following the sign 'Ridge Path for Rollington Hill'. As you walk, wide views unfold, north over Studland Heath and the Inland Sea to Poole harbour, and south over a valley dotted with small villages and farms to the final seaward-facing ridge of the Purbeck Hills.

Corfe Castle – *The Greyhound Inn*

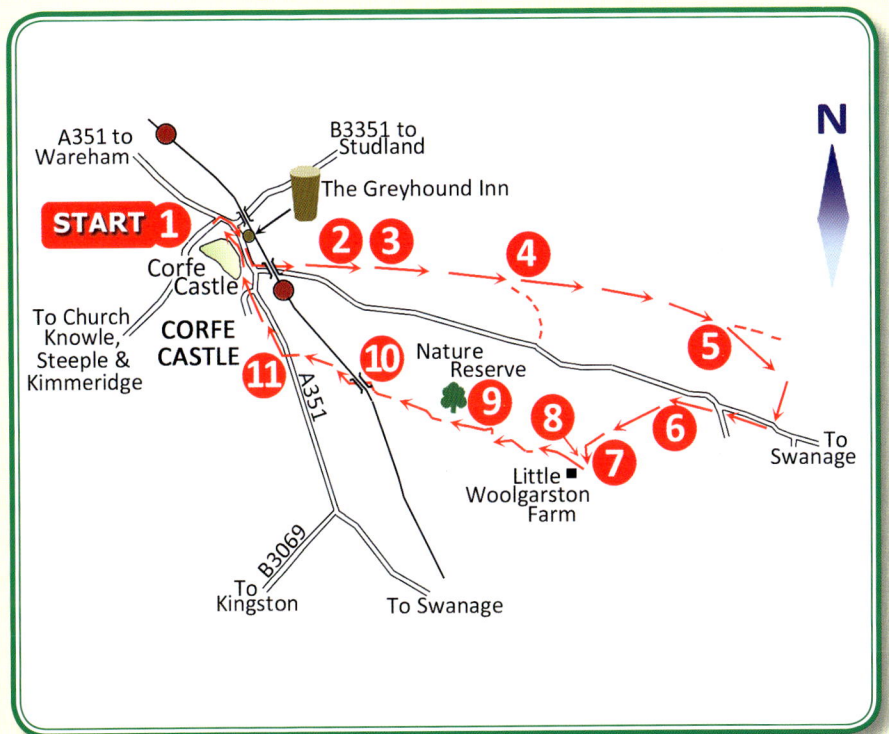

4 Pass a tall mast on your left, go through a gate, and follow the path bearing a little left uphill. Pass the stone marked 'Little Woolgarston'. Keep ahead over the down for about a mile to Brenscombe Hill and the next stone marked just 'Woolgarston'.

5 Turn right and follow the track downhill through a gate. The track bears a little right to bring you to a lane. Turn right and follow the lane for about ¼ mile to a footpath on the left signed 'Little Woolgarston'.

6 Turn left over a stile and bear a little left down the field to cross double stiles. Continue over the next field following the direction of the yellow arrow footpath sign. Climb more double stiles, cross the field ahead, and go over a stile and a wooden footbridge. A path leads through the trees to go up steps to a lane.

Pub Walks in Dorset

ASCENDING THE DOWN TO ROLLINGTON HILL

7. Turn left, go through the gate of Little Woolgarston Farm and after a few yards turn right through a gate following the sign 'Corfe Castle 2'.

8. There is no path at this point but walk up the hill to a gate on the top a few yards to your left opening into the National Trust owned nature reserve. Follow the path downhill and continue with a hedge on your right. The path bears half-left downhill past a post supporting power cables.

9. Keep to the same path as it curves right past a green arrowed National Trust sign, runs a little uphill, then bears left with a fence about 30 yards away on the right.

10. The path drops downhill to take you along a boardwalk, through a gate and under the railway. Go through the next gate and bear right following the direction of a green arrow. The path winds beside a meadow, then between hedges before dropping downhill to cross a stream. Keep straight ahead past a path on the right and go through a gate to Corfe Castle village.

Corfe Castle – *The Greyhound Inn*

11 Turn right to walk through the village to the Square and the Greyhound Inn. Turn left across the Square then follow the sign pointing right to the Castle entrance. Go past a barrier and cross the bridge over the moat. Just before the gateway to the castle look for a narrow footpath on your right leading through a small gate marked by a National Trust sign. Turn right through the gate and follow the path leading round the castle mound with the ramparts on your left. Go through a gate at the foot of the mound and cross the road to your car.

PLACE OF INTEREST NEARBY

Corfe Castle is an imposing ruin dating from the time of William the Conqueror. In AD 978 Queen Elfrida poisoned and stabbed her stepson King Edward outside the gate. During the Civil War the castle stood for the king and was heroically defended by Lady Bankes. It fell to the Parliamentary forces owing to the treachery of one of the defenders. The castle was slighted in 1646 soon after its capture. The castle is open daily for most of the year but times vary. ∅ (infoline): 01929 477060; postcode BH20 5EZ

Lytchett Minster
St Peters Finger
4½ miles (7.2 km)

Although so close to Poole, Lytchett Minster is a real country village. Cottages and houses, many thatched, are set among green fields and woods. The small church, at the heart of the community, is flooded with light from a beautiful east window installed to commemorate Queen Victoria's Diamond Jubilee. The surrounding countryside is threaded with narrow lanes and tree-bordered footpaths.

From the pub you follow a country lane then head north taking footpaths which dip through oak and pine woods to bring you to Lytchett Matravers. The route turns south along a quiet lane giving wide views over the

Lytchett Minster – *St Peters Finger*

3

Solent to the Isle of Wight. You return to Lytchett Minster along another woodland footpath which rejoins part of the outbound route. You can follow an alternative road past South Lytchett manor house, an elegant Georgian mansion which unfortunately has suffered from fire. It is now a comprehensive school. (N.B. For security reasons, the road past the school is gated after seven in the evening.)

The **ST PETERS FINGER** is a friendly, warm-hearted pub as attractive as the village. Its unusual name is explained on the wall outside. According to legend, St Peter once caught a fish with a gold coin in its mouth and now thieves are said to have fish hooks in their fingers! The pub is light and spacious, with plenty of room for families and cosy alcoves if you wish to tuck yourself away in a quiet corner. There is also a lovely beer garden at the back as well as a small courtyard terrace. The staff take real pleasure in making you feel at home and they ensure you enjoy your visit. The menus provide a wide range of traditional dishes, with sandwiches, sharing plates and larger main courses all available, and all of which can be followed by a delicious selection of desserts.

✆ 01202 622 275; postcode BH16 6JE

> **How to get there:** The best approach is via the A35. Turn for Lytchett Minster along the B3067, pass the Bakers Arms pub on your right and shortly after turn right into the St Peters Finger car park.
> **Parking:** St Peters Finger car park.
> **Map:** OS Explorer 118 Shaftesbury and Cranborne Chase (South Sheet) (GR: SY961929).

THE WALK

1 Cross the road in front of the pub and follow New Road. This soon becomes a quiet lane with grass verges leading through meadows. Continue along the lane as it bears a little right at a junction, following the sign for Lytchett Matravers and Post Green. Pass the farm at Post Green on your left.

2 When the lane curves sharply right, keep straight ahead along the bridleway past a large iron gate. Follow the hedged path ahead with a wood on your right.

Pub Walks in Dorset

3 At the corner of the wood the path swings left to run under the arching branches of oak trees. You pass a thick wood on your left. A large fallow deer with its distinctive white rump bounded across my path to disappear into the wood! The path dips downhill to cross a stream.

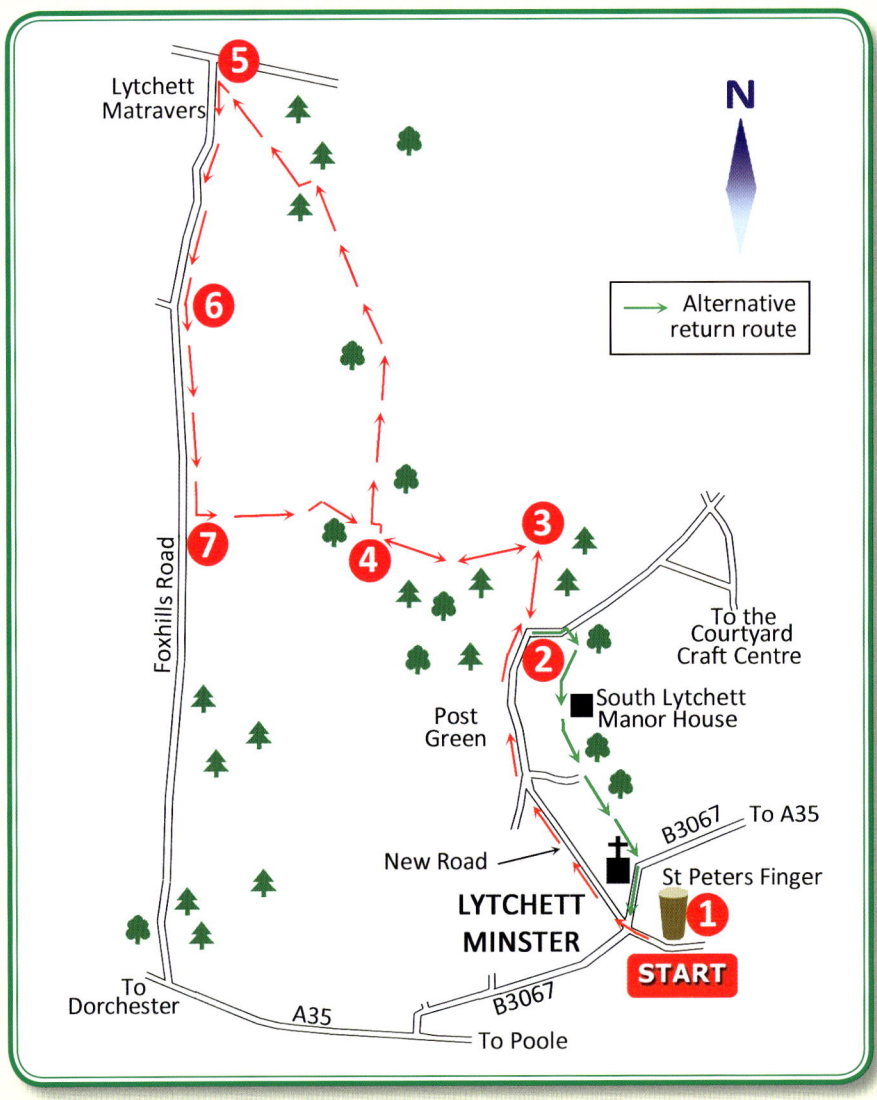

Lytchett Minster – *St Peters Finger*

4 Keep ahead for about 50 yards then turn right to walk up to a gate. Turn left just before the gate, continue ahead for about 50 yards then turn right to follow a path with a fence on your right and a pine wood on your left. The path rises gently and looking back you can see over the woods and the silver glint of the Solent to the Isle of Wight. The path curves left past a gate on the right. A few yards further on keep ahead past a narrow path on your right to a signed footpath. Turn right to follow this clear path with a wood on your right and a hedge on your left. The path continues past stables to emerge in Foxhills Road on the outskirts of Lytchett Matravers.

5 Turn left along the pavement and follow the road for about ½ mile.

6 At this point the road you are following curves sharply right. (This is not obvious on the map.) Do not follow the road round but keep straight on down the narrow unsigned road ahead bordered by fields. Looking south there are more wide-ranging views to the Isle of Wight hills. Just before a wood you come to a bridleway sign on your left.

7 Turn left to follow this attractive path which drops downhill and curves right through oak woods. A tiny stream runs along beside you on your right. Keep ahead past a track on the left to pass a gate and meet the outbound route at point 4. Retrace your steps until you meet New Road at point 2. If you wish you could continue along New Road to return to the village but to see the manor turn left for a short distance along the road. Turn right along the drive to the school which runs past the manor and the school buildings. Go through the gates at the end of the drive and turn right past the church to return to the pub.

PLACE OF INTEREST NEARBY

The **Courtyard Craft Centre** is close to Lytchett Minster and is well worth a visit. Entry and parking are free and crafts on display include pottery, photography and jewellery. Classes are on offer. There is a medieval hall and an excellent restaurant. The Centre is open every day including Sundays and Bank Holidays. ✆ 01202 631030; postcode BH16 6BA

Corfe Mullen (Lambs Green)
The Lambs Green Inn
3 miles (4.8 km)

This beautiful walk is within a stone's throw of the outskirts of Poole. For almost the whole way you follow footpaths leading through oak and beech woods full of wild flowers and birdsong.

The walk starts in Lambs Green where the northern outskirts of Corfe Mullen overlook the Stour valley. The lane from the inn leads to a path which crosses the track of the disused Somerset and Dorset railway to enter woodland. The path descends to follow a track beside the route of a Roman road. You leave the road to explore the heathland of Corfe Hills

Corfe Mullen – *The Lambs Green Inn*

Nature Reserve before returning to Lambs Green along a footpath which dips across a valley intriguingly named Happy Bottom!

The **LAMBS GREEN INN** is a charming inn that was once a farm. The thatched cottage and its tasteful extension retain the original rural atmosphere, with a massive fireplace, flagged and tiled floors and beamed alcoves. The added benefit of a large beer garden makes this pub deservedly popular. You'll find a large seasonal menu full of hearty favourites along with lighter bites. Options include steaks, burgers, pizzas, salads and sandwiches so most appetite sizes are catered for. There is also a well stocked bar offering cask ales, fine wines and British gin.
✆ 01202 881974; postcode BH21 3DN

How to get there: Approaching from the west along the A31, pass the Coventry Arms pub on your left and a sign for Corfe Mullen and Broadstone. Continue to the next traffic island and turn left following the sign for Corfe Mullen. After ¼ mile turn left into Lambs Green Lane. The inn is on the corner. Approaching from the east, follow the Wimborne bypass (A31) to the traffic island and turn left following a sign on the left for Corfe Mullen. After ¼ mile turn left into Lambs Green Lane as above.
Parking: The Lambs Green Inn car park.
Map: OS Explorer 118 Shaftesbury and Cranborne Chase (South Sheet) (GR SY997988).

THE WALK

1. Turn left from the front door of the Lambs Green Inn to follow Lambs Green Lane.

2. After about 400 yards, just before the lane curves left, turn right along a tree-bordered path following the bridleway sign passing a chapel-like building on your left. The path leads to a brick bridge over the disused railway. The Somerset and Dorset railway connecting Bath with Bournemouth opened in 1872.

3. Cross the bridge and continue over a track. Take the narrow bridleway ahead, with a fence at first on your left. This becomes an attractive

path with woodland rising on your right. Pass a path on your right. When the path begins to drop downhill, leave it, and **turn right** uphill through the woods. Shortly the path descends to a crosspath.

4. Turn left and follow the path over a stream. The path rises to a road. Cross the road, turn right for a few yards then turn left to follow the bridleway signed for Upton.

The overgrown bank leading beside the track on your left is part of a road built by the Roman Second Legion under Vespasian. They arrived in the Corfe Mullen area around AD 40. From their deep water anchorage at Hamworthy the road runs north to their forts at Badbury Rings and Hod Hill. During the 18th and early years of the 19th century when smuggling luxury goods from France was rife, this long straight road provided a convenient path for the smugglers to follow at night. It now forms the boundary between Corfe Mullen and Broadstone.

5. Keep ahead past a track on the left to step over a low metal barrier. A few yards further on leave the Roman road and turn left along a path over the heath of Corfe Hills Nature Reserve. (This is unsigned at present but the reserve is open access land.)

6. When you meet a crosspath turn left along another attractive woodland path. Beyond the trees on your right the heath dips to a wide valley dotted with pines. Pass some stables and keep ahead along a tarmac lane.

7. Turn left along the lane to a road.

8. Bear right to cross a bridge over the disused railway then turn left along Ashington Lane. Follow the lane for about ¼ mile to a gate and footpath sign on your left signed 'Happy Bottom'.

9. Go through the gate and follow the track downhill through the trees into this small bowl-shaped valley. The track leads to a gate opening into fields. Do not go through the gate but turn right just before it to follow a fenced path which weaves round the valley. Cross a small wooden footbridge, go through a gate and climb the hill ahead to go through another gate.

Corfe Mullen – *The Lambs Green Inn*

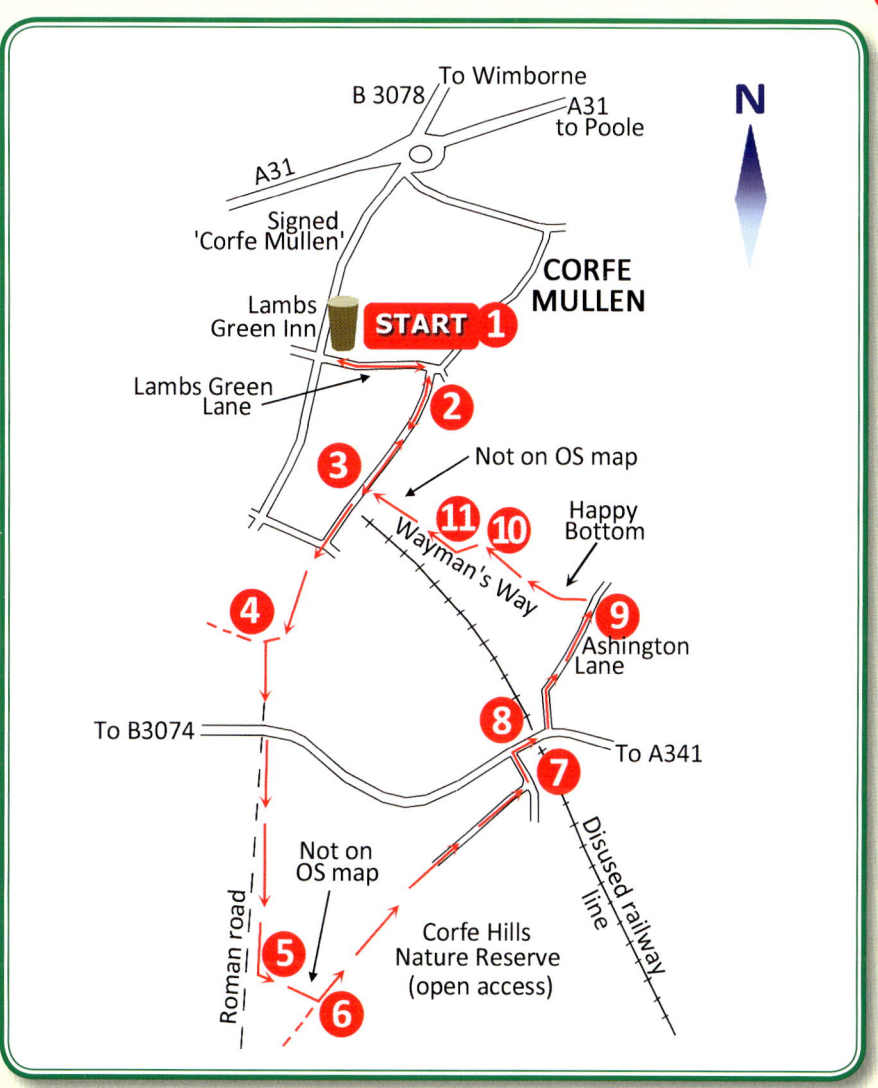

10. Turn left through the woods to go through a gate to a junction of several paths.

11. Turn right following the path along the top of the disused railway

Pub Walks in Dorset

embankment signed 'Wayman's Way'. We owe this attractive path (which was not marked on our OS map) to Charles Wayman who once owned this land and wished other people to enjoy it. The Way meets a path you followed outbound. Turn right to retrace your steps along the path and turn left to return to the Lambs Green Inn.

Early spring in Happy Bottom

PLACE OF INTEREST NEARBY

Walford Mill lies beside the river Allen, ¼ mile north of Wimborne Minster, a short walk from the town centre. The mill, which is run by the Dorset Crafts Guild, features work by local, national and international craft workers. There is a licensed café. Entry is free. ✆ 01202 841400; postcode BH21 1NL

Horton
The Horton Inn
5¼ miles (8.4 km)

Horton is a small village tucked in the downs on the southern fringe of Cranborne Chase. From the village a gentle climb takes you to Horton Tower. Known locally as 'Sturt's Folly', this hexagonal six-storeyed brick tower was erected by Humphrey Sturt, an 18th-century landowner, so that he could watch the hunt when he became too infirm to ride.

———•••———

A quiet lane leads you to one of the loveliest places on the chase, the tiny white-walled church at Chalbury. The return route follows tracks high over the downs with wide views before taking a sunken woodland path downhill into Horton valley. A path through wildflower meadows leads you back to the village.

Pub Walks in Dorset

The **HORTON INN** is a traditional country pub and hotel where walkers are made to feel very welcome. In the bar you'll find a cosy atmosphere with sofas and an open fire, and there is a large dining area where a wide range of homemade food is on offer. Most of the usual pub favourites are on the menu, along with some vegetarian and vegan choices.
✆ 01258 840252; postcode BH21 5AD

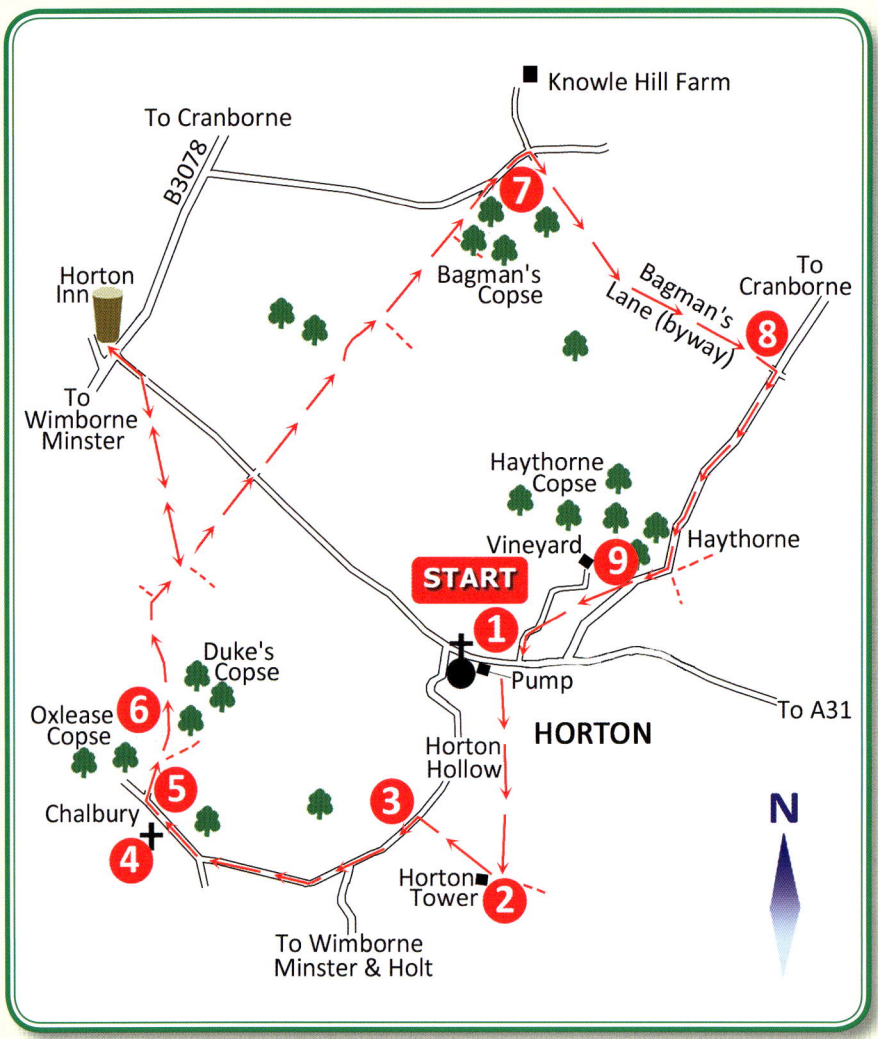

HORTON – *The Horton Inn*

5

> **How to get there:** There is a lay-by just near the village hall on the main road through the village.
> **Parking:** Lay-by on Horton Road.
> **Map:** OS Explorer 118 Shaftesbury and Cranborne Chase (South Sheet) (GR: SU039074).

THE WALK

1 Turn right from the lay-by to walk towards Horton. As you approach the village, you will see a pump sheltered by a pyramid-shaped roof. To the left of the pump a footpath sign points uphill towards Horton Tower. Turn left, following the sign, to climb the hill crossing two stiles. There is no clear path but aim just to the left of the tower avoiding a wide hollow on your right. In Saxon times an abbey was built here and the hollow is said to be haunted! The village church is dedicated to St Wolfrida, an abbess who died in Horton.

2 At the top of the hill turn right passing the tower on your left. Follow the ridge path through a gate and an oak copse to a drive. Bear left for a few yards to meet Chalbury Lane.

3 Turn left along the lane past the Chalbury Common sign. At a junction the lane curves left by a signpost. Follow the right-hand lane straight ahead signed for Chalbury Hill. The lane rises a little and curves right past a lane on the left. Between the trees on your right you can look north over Cranborne Chase to the Wiltshire Downs.

4 As you approach the few scattered houses of Chalbury village, look for a flight of steps on your left. Climb the steps which lead to Chalbury church. This tiny church, dating from the 13th century, stands alone on the hilltop. It is beautifully cared for. Inside, the nave is lined with high-sided box pews overlooked by an old wooden gallery. From the churchyard there is a magnificent view south over the Stour valley and the Purbeck Hills to the Channel and the Isle of Wight.

Descend the steps and turn left to continue along the lane.

5 After about 100 yards turn right following the bridleway sign for Horton. The bridleway drops downhill through a gate past trees on your left to lead through the woods of Oxleaze Copse and Duke's

Pub Walks in Dorset

Copse. Perhaps Duke's Copse owes its name to the ill-fated Duke of Monmouth who, after fleeing from the battlefield at Sedgemoor, was discovered hiding in a ditch near Horton.

6 As the trees thin, you are faced with two farm gates. Go through the left-hand gate and keep ahead beside a meadow with a hedge on your right. The next gate opens to a wide track leading north-east over the downs bordered by hedges rich in wildflowers. Follow the track past Chalbury Farm on your left. To detour to the pub, cross the field to your left, just past the farm buildings, and head to the opposite corner. Enter the next field to your left and head towards the far corner where you will find a stile leading to the road. Climb the stile, turn left and you will see the Horton Inn directly ahead of you. Retrace your steps to continue the walk. If you're not visiting the pub, keep ahead along the track away from Chalbury Farm, cross straight over the minor road to Horton and keep ahead to continue past North Farm on your right through the farm gates. The track runs through Bagman's Copse to a lane. Turn right to walk along the lane for about 150 yards.

7 After passing some overgrown farm buildings on your right, look carefully for a byway sign on your right leading into woodland. It is opposite a lane to Knowle Hill Farm. Turn right, following the byway sign, to follow a track known as Bagman's Lane through the woods. The track sinks deep below the tree roots canopied with waving branches and bordered with ferns. It is easy to imagine the weary duke seeking a refuge in these mysterious woodlands. The track leaves the wood to become a grassy path running between hedges to a minor road.

Horton – *The Horton Inn*

8 Turn right to follow the road through Haythorne, a small cluster of houses half-hidden in trees. Just past a Horton village sign, look for a footpath sign for Horton on your right.

HORTON VILLAGE

9 Turn right to follow the path leading through the trees of Haythorne Copse going downhill through the meadows to meet the lane to Horton Estate Vineyard. Pass the gates of the vineyard and, bearing left, follow the lane to the road. Turn left to return to your car.

PLACE OF INTEREST NEARBY

Horton Estate Vineyard produces white, red and sparkling wines. The courtyard shop is open at weekends from 10am to 4pm for tasting and sales. ✆ 01258 840258; postcode BH21 7JG

Iwerne Courtney
The Cricketers
2½ miles (4 km)

An easy climb from Iwerne Courtney brings you to the top of Hambledon Hill, an outlying spur of chalk downland crowned with the embankments of a great iron age fort. From this vantage point there are spectacular view west over the Blackmoor Vale, east over Iwerne Valley and the slopes of Cranborne Chase, and south over the coast to the Isle of Wight.

This short stroll is proof that you do not need to walk far to enjoy some of the finest scenery this lovely county has to offer. The route follows the Wessex Ridgeway with views of Hod Hill, also ringed by the embankments of an Iron Age fort, before we return along the valley to our starting point near The Cricketers pub.

THE CRICKETERS is situated in the shadow of Hambledon Hill in the heart of one of Dorset's prettiest villages. As its name suggests it is close to the village's beautifully maintained cricket pitch and the cricketing theme is

Iwerne Courtney – *The Cricketers*

6

very much in evidence. Spacious alcoves contribute to the pub's restful and relaxed atmosphere. The menu features a wide choice of dishes with some delicious daily specials available. Produce is locally sourced and fresh fish is delivered daily.

The pub is popular so if you plan a group visit let the owner know beforehand so that everything can be ready for you.

✆ 01258 268107; postcode DT11 8QD

> **How to get there:** Iwerne Courtney (also called Shroton) lies just west of the A350 Blandford Forum-Shaftesbury Road, about 5 miles north of Blandford Forum. Heading north turn left for Iwerne Courtney and follow the road round as it bends right to the church on your left and a large parking area on your right.
> **Parking:** Parking area opposite the church.
> **Map:** OS Explorer 118 Shaftesbury & Cranborne Chase (GR: ST860124).

THE WALK

1 With the parking area on your right and the church on your left, walk up the village street for a few yards then turn left along Fairfield Road, passing a massive thatched barn on your left. The road curves right towards the cricket pavilion. Just before the pavilion you will see a bridleway sign on the left. Take this path.

2 With the cricket pitch on your right, turn half-left and head up the hill towards a stone wall.

3 Go through a metal gate.

4 A few yards further on, turn right and walk up the side of a field to go through another metal gate. Continue uphill. The track leads up to a trig point on the crest of the ridge. The world of Blackmoor Vale is spread before you.

5 Our way is left at the trig point. But first you might like to turn right to the embankments of Hambledon Hill Iron Age fort. You will be rewarded with more splendid views and a wealth of wild flowers in

Pub Walks in Dorset

IWERNE COURTNEY FROM THE PATH TO HAMBLEDON HILL

season. Retrace your steps to the trig point and keep straight on along the ridge between fences, passing the top of our earlier path on the left. Ahead rise the ramparts of the Iron Age fort on Hod Hill. The track descends and curves right through a gate. The humps and bumps in the field on your right are the grass-covered remains of a Neolithic camp dating back to around 2,790 BC.

6 Leave the Wessex Ridgeway here. From the gate the path bears left for a few yards then right to run along the foot of a hill with a wood on the left. (Ignore the parallel track closer to the wood.) Follow the path through gates until you come to a large iron barn. Keep to the path leading steeply downhill to a small wooden gate on the left. Turn left through the gate and follow the narrow path ahead through another

Iwerne Courtney – *The Cricketers*

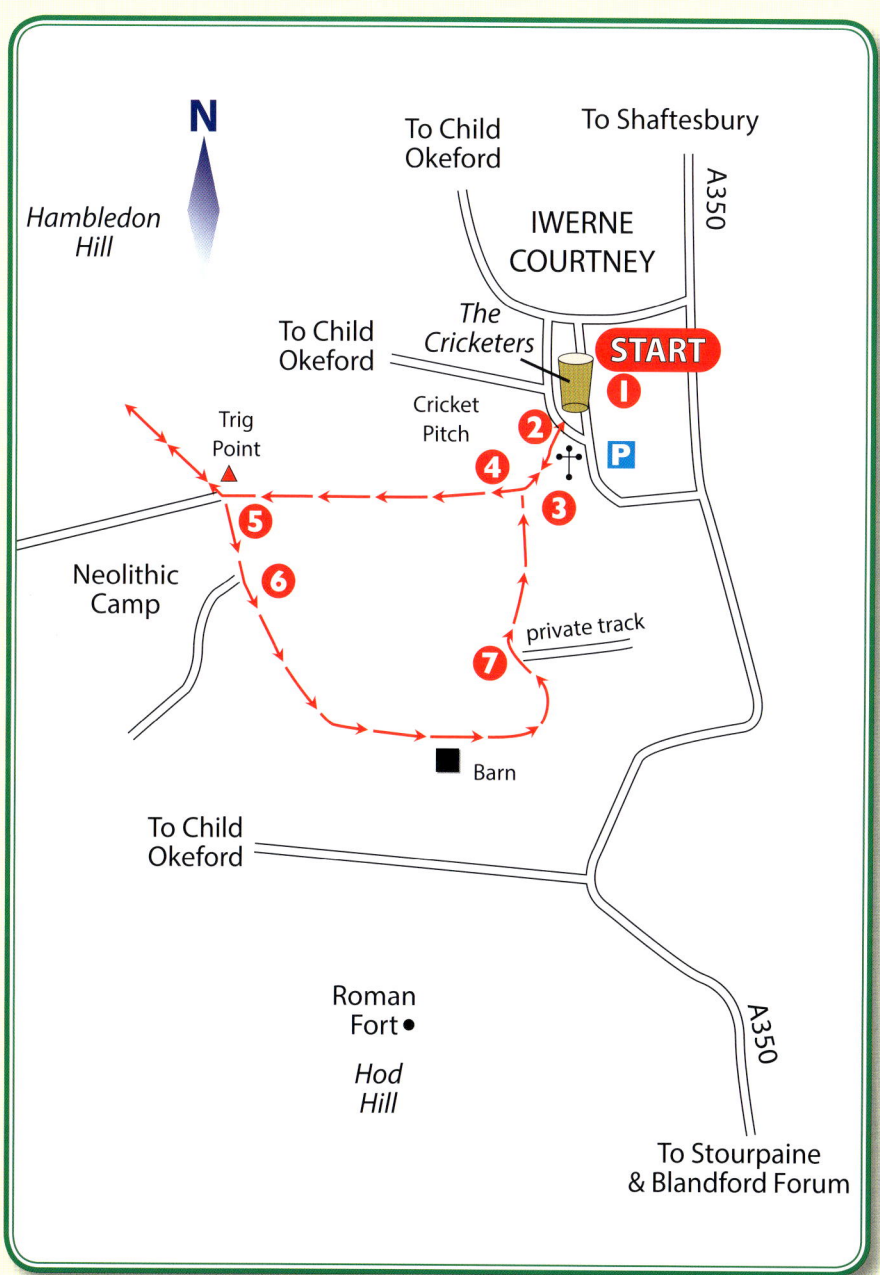

Pub Walks in Dorset

gate and continue along the hillside, passing a wood and 'Private Track' sign on your right.

7 The track widens here, dipping and rising along the foot of a field to bring you back to the metal gate at point 3. Bear left to retrace your steps past the cricket pitch. Turn right to follow Fairfield Road back to the High Street. Turn left to walk the few yards to The Cricketers or right to return to your car..

PLACE OF INTEREST NEARBY

Hod Hill, owned by the National Trust, is a well-preserved Roman fort within Iron Age embankments and is renowned for its rare plants and butterflies. Best approached on foot from Stourpaine.
 ⌀ postcode DT11 8TA

MALE COMMON BLUE BUTTERFLY ON HOD HILL

Tarrant Gunville
Home Farm
4½ miles (7.2 km)

Hidden away in the north of Cranborne Chase, the little River Tarrant flows south for ten miles carving a beautiful valley through the downs. You start this walk in Tarrant Gunville, a charming village with many attractive thatched cottages, close to the source of the river.

After heading west past the church of St Mary, you turn south along the first of the woodland ways which are a feature of this walk. Field paths lead you back to the Tarrant. Over the river, you follow more tree-shaded paths across the parkland surrounding Eastbury House, the converted kitchen block of a once-great 18th-century mansion. Designed by Vanburgh for George Bubb Doddington, 1st Baron Melcombe, the mansion proved so large that no one wanted to live in it. So, apart from the kitchen block and the impressive gateways, it was demolished. But today the parkland and its fine trees provide a memorable finish to your walk.

Pub Walks in Dorset

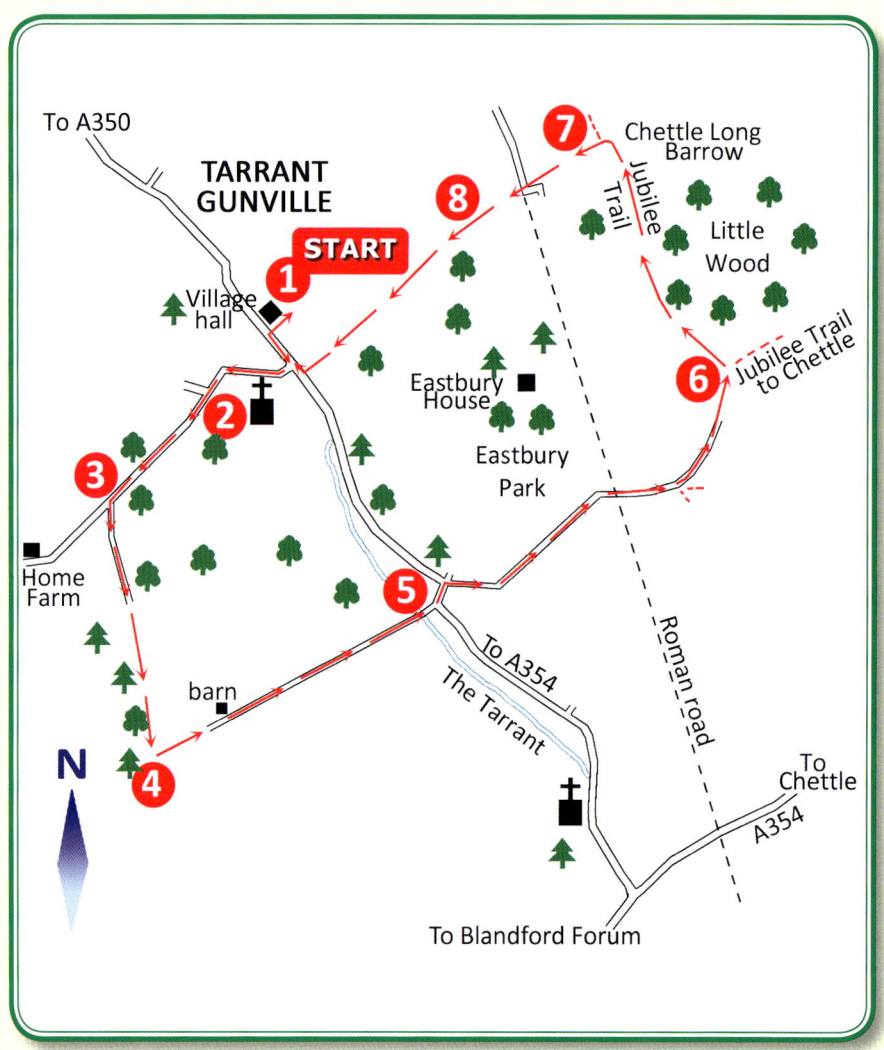

HOME FARM is signed from the village and close to the route of the walk. The restaurant has a wine licence and is open all the year. You can sample delicious teas, indulge in a real farmhouse-kitchen breakfast, choose from a wide range of sandwiches and baguettes or enjoy a light lunch. The farm shop is stocked with locally produced foods.

✆ 01258 830083; postcode DT11 8JW

TARRANT GUNVILLE – *Home Farm*

7

How to get there: Tarrant Gunville is best approached via the A354 Blandford Forum–Salisbury road. Turn right for Tarrant Hinton and continue up the valley for about 1½ miles to Tarrant Gunville. Just past the phone box on the left, turn right leaving the village hall on your left to park by the road.
Parking: Roadside parking as indicated above.
Map: OS Explorer 118 Shaftesbury and Cranborne Chase (GR: ST925129).

THE WALK

1. Turn left from the village hall to walk down the road with the Tarrant stream on your left. You pass the old forge on your right. The yellow AA plaque on the wall gives information for motorists recalling the early days when the AA was responsible for road signs.

    Turn right following the sign for the church and Everley Hill. Pass the church parking area and a few yards further on gates on the left lead to a footpath to the church. The church has a fine 15th-century tower and some interesting 16th-century stained glass which includes the arms of Henry VIII and two of his wives.

2. Continue along the lane and at the road junction keep straight ahead following the sign for Home Farm.

3. After about ½ mile you will see a large white sign for Home Farm (which is further down the road) on your left and a post marked with a blue bridleway arrow indicating a broad track on your left leading into woods. Turn left and follow the track bordered by many fine beech and oak trees. Keep straight ahead past a track on the left along a narrow path leading through coppiced woodland. The path continues past a gate to dip downhill then rises to run beside a field to meet a gravelled track.

4. Turn left – you will see the roof of a barn in the valley ahead – and walk beside a field with a hedge on your right. Pass the barn on your left and follow the track ahead to meet the Tarrant Valley road.

5. Take care here! Turn left beside the road for about 50 yards then turn

Pub Walks in Dorset

right up the 'No Through Road'. The enormous trees of Eastbury Park are on your left. The road becomes a beautiful tree-shaded track. Keep to the track as it bears a little left past bridleway and footpath signs on the right. Over the fields on your right there are wide views over Cranborne Chase.

6 The track enters the trees of Little Wood and after a few yards divides just past a gate. At this point you join the Jubilee Trail marked by a green and yellow sign. Turn left to follow the Jubilee Trail through Little Wood. (Ignore the track straight ahead which leads to Chettle.) Leave the wood to continue beside a field with trees on your left. After about ¼ mile you pass the mound of Chettle Long Barrow raised by the first people to farm these downs in the New Stone Age.

7 Just past the Long Barrow turn left following the Jubilee Trail sign over a stile. The path curves left then right, then follows the field edge with a hedge on the left. You come to a narrow asphalt track. At this point the track is on the route of a Roman road that ran south from the Wiltshire border down the Tarrant Valley on its way to Badbury Rings and Poole Harbour. Cross the track and keep ahead along the grassy track.

8 The track turns left over a stile. Turn immediately right along the narrow path with a hedge on the right leading along the edge of Eastbury Park. An avenue of magnificent trees crosses the parkland on your left and beyond them you will see Eastbury House, all that remains of Vanburgh's great mansion. Follow the path round to the left to go through a gate and bear right through a wood to a lane. Follow the lane to the Tarrant Valley road and turn right to return to the village hall in Tarrant Gunville and your car.

PLACE OF INTEREST NEARBY

The **Larmer Tree Gardens**, historic gardens created by General Pitt Rivers in 1880, are about 6 miles east of Tarrant Gunville, near Tollard Royal. These stunning gardens contain oriental-inspired buildings and ponds, as well as free-flying macaws and roaming peacocks. There is free parking and a café. The gardens are open Sunday to Wednesday 11am to 4.30pm, but check the website for closures due to private events. ✆ 01725 516971; postcode SP5 5PT

Tarrant Keyneston
True Lovers Knot
4 miles (6.4 km)

This enchanting walk follows the little River Tarrant through beautiful downland close to the river's confluence with the Stour to Tarrant Crawford. Once the site of a flourishing cistercian abbey, all that remains of the village today is a farm, a few cottages and Tarrant Abbey House, close to the abbey ruins. The tiny church of St Mary the Virgin, set among the trees on the hillside is one of Dorset's gems.

The walk starts from the True Lovers Knot pub in Tarrant Keyneston. You take the lane through this attractive village, then cross the river to

Pub Walks in Dorset

follow a riverside footpath to the most southerly of the Tarrant villages, Tarrant Crawford. From its church you follow downland paths, with wide views over the Tarrant valley, before retracing your steps through Tarrant Keyneston to the pub.

The **TRUE LOVERS KNOT** is a traditional country pub that offers a warm welcome to all and the enthusiastic staff make sure you enjoy your visit. The name of the pub acts as a magnet for lovers and evidently many proposals take place in the restaurant. No one is quite sure how the pub got its name but the most popular belief concerns a tragic love affair. Once upon a time the landlord's son fell in love with the local lord's daughter. Horrified, her father threatened to send her away whereupon she hanged herself from a tree. Her grieving boyfriend hanged himself from the same tree. The landlord could not bear the loss of his son and also hanged himself from the tree. The locals referred to the inn as the True Lovers Knot because the knot has three loops and a heart in the middle. Today the pub is said to be haunted by the tragic landlord but there is nothing spooky about the locally brewed real ales or the delicious food which is also locally sourced. There are plenty of pub classics on offer along with a separate lunch menu with smaller dishes including sandwiches and jacket potatoes.

The pub offers accommodation.

✆ 01258 452209; postcode DT11 9JG

How to get there: The True Lovers Knot faces the B3082 between Blandford Forum and Wimborne Minster.
Parking: In the pub car park.
Map: OS Explorer 118 Shaftesbury and Cranborne Chase (GR: ST933047).

THE WALK

1 Leave the front door of the True Lovers Knot, cross the road and follow the lane immediately ahead leading through Tarrant Keyneston village.

You pass a venerable thatched house, The Old Post Office, on your right. All Saints church has retained its medieval tower which houses a 14th-century tenor bell.

Tarrant Keyneston – *True Lovers Knot* 8

Approaching the historic church at Tarrant Crawford

2 Continue past the church and after about 150 yards, turn left following the sign 'Bridleway to Tarrant Crawford'. The footpath crosses a small bridge over the Tarrant where the clear water splashes over a weir. Follow the narrow path ahead which bears right along the valley. The stream is on your right.

3 Pass a track leading up the hillside on your left. Here the return route rejoins the riverside path.

4 The path widens as you approach Tarrant Crawford church. Walk past the church to enter the churchyard through a small gate.

The tiny church of St Mary the Virgin is Grade I listed, and dates from the 12th century. An outstanding feature is a series of 14th-century wall paintings. Queen Joanna, the wife of Alexander II of Scotland, is buried in the churchyard.

Before the abbey was built, a house adjoining the church was the home of three aristocratic ladies called Anchoresses. They wished to lead a religious life but to follow no established rule so Bishop Poore wrote a guide for them, the Ancren Riwle. Although the ladies were to lead a strict religious life, the kindly bishop advises their clothes should be warm and well-made and allows them to keep a cat.

After visiting the church, return through the gate and keep straight ahead along the track which after a few yards is barred by a large iron gate.

5. Just before the large gate, turn left through a small gate marked with a blue arrow bridleway sign and bear half-left diagonally up the hillside. (You will see the path more clearly as it runs through the trees near the top of the hill.) You pass a quarry on your left.

6. At the top of the hill go through a gate. Keep ahead across a meadow following the line of wires and go through a gate to a road.

7. Cross the road and go through a small gate. Bear left down a meadow keeping a fence close on your left to a road junction by a wayside cross.

8. Turn left passing the cross on your right. Follow the sign for Shapwick for only a few yards then leave the road and take the hedged track on your left which leads gently uphill to pass an iron barn on the right.

9. About 200 yards past the barn turn left along a similar hedged track which slowly descends the hillside to rejoin your outbound route by the riverside at point 3. Turn right to retrace your steps, with the river now on your left, to cross the bridge and walk up the lane as far as the church.

10. Just after the church turn left up a track past a house on your right, then turn right to follow a footpath which leads over stiles to a road in a housing estate. Cross straight over and follow the footpath ahead until you come to a stile leading into fields. The path ahead is not clear so I recommend you turn right here to walk down to the lane. Turn left to retrace your steps through the village and cross the road to the True Lovers Knot.

Tarrant Keyneston – *True Lovers Knot*   8

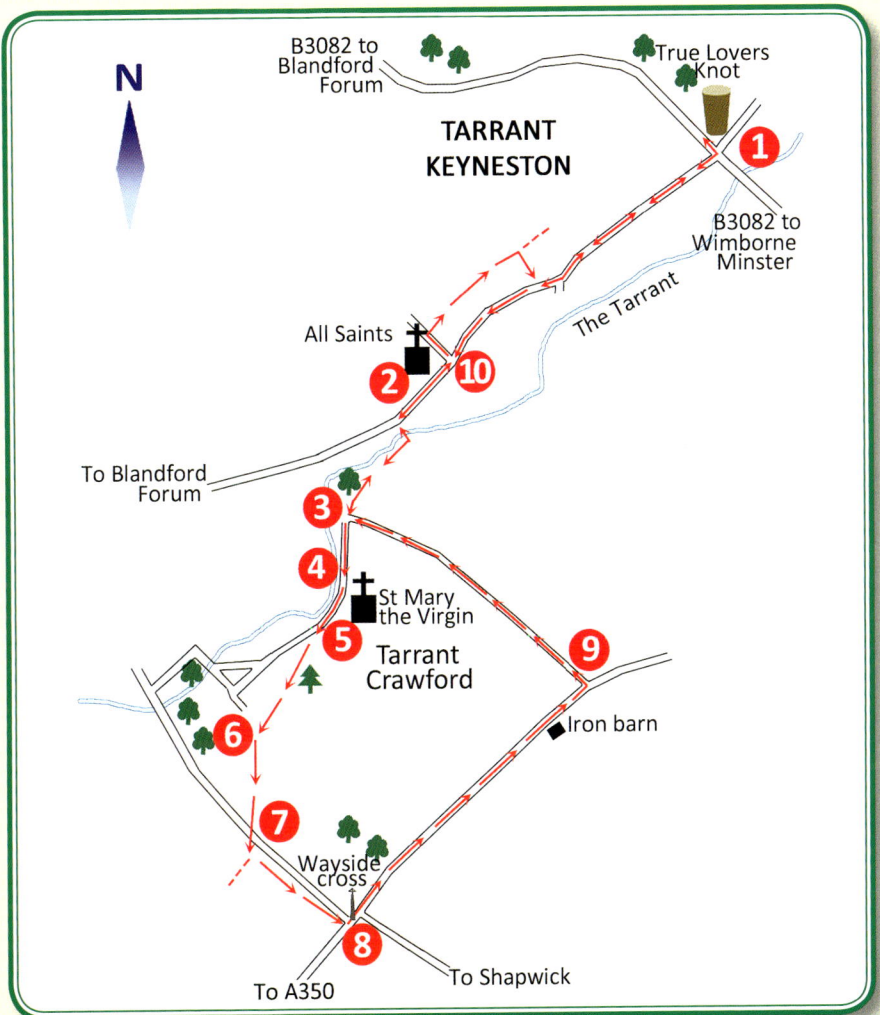

PLACE OF INTEREST NEARBY

A mile west of the village is the botanic garden at **Keyneston Mill**. Book a scented garden tour or workshop, or simply enjoy roaming the garden and a visit to the café and gift shop.
✆ 01258 786022; postcode DT11 9DF

45

Winterborne Zelston
The Botany Bay Inne
4 miles (6.4 km)

As you follow the route of this walk down the lane opposite the pub, past the thatched and white-walled houses of Winterborne Zelston into the Winterborne Valley, you will discover Dorset at its most appealing.

The lane loses itself in wide lawns beside the little Winterborne stream crossed at intervals by small brick bridges. From the village you take meadow paths heading west to Winterborne Tomson. Now just a farm and a few scattered houses it is believed to be one of Dorset's lost villages. More meadow paths lead you to Winterborne Anderson with its magnificent manor house. The return route follows the course of a Roman road and runs through woods full of wild flowers before descending to Winterborne Zelston on a quiet lane.

The **BOTANY BAY INNE** is a large family pub. The inn was built in the 1920s by Hall and Woodhouse on land given by the local squire. He had

Winterborne Zelston – *The Botany Bay Inne*

the pub moved from the village as he did not like looking at it! At the time the pub was called 'The General Allenby' but the name was changed in the 1980s to commemorate the first convicts on their way from Dorchester prison to take ship at Portsmouth for Botany Bay. They spent the night nearby at Bloxworth farm. The red signpost you pass just before the pub marks the turning to the farm. Those who were struggling at this point were hanged!

Luckily, these days all you'll find is a beautiful country pub serving delicious home cooked food.

✆ 01929 459227; postcode DT11 9ET

> **How to get there:** Winterborne Zelston is just off the A31 between Wimborne Minster and Bere Regis. The Botany Bay Inne is on the south side of the A31 overlooking the lane to the village.
> **Parking:** The Botany Bay car park.
> **Map:** OS Explorer 117 Cerne Abbas and Bere Regis (GR: SY899974).

THE WALK

1 Cross the road in front of the pub and walk down the lane following the sign for Winterborne Zelston. At the foot of the lane turn right with the stream on your left. You pass the base of a Saxon preaching cross which was re-erected in 1977 to celebrate the Queen's Silver Jubilee. Follow the lane as it curves left over a small brick bridge. The bridge is a favourite place for playing Pooh Sticks and if you have forgotten how to play it, you will find guidance on a plaque on the parapet! Pass the church on your right and a few yards further on turn left following the footpath sign for Winterborne Kingston.

2 The track leads past the village hall. Go through a wooden gate to walk beside a meadow with a fence then a hedge on your left. Continue through a metal gate and cross the next meadow to go through another metal gate in front of some farm buildings.

3 Continue for a few yards past the first of the farm buildings. Then turn right to walk between the buildings. After about 50 yards, turn left to pass more farm buildings and a house on your left to continue heading west along an attractive lane fringed with trees. This leads

Pub Walks in Dorset

to a cross-track. (The present route round the farm differs from the OS map.)

4. Turn left to walk past the farm at Winterborne Tomson built in the 17th century with massive gables and tall clustered chimneys. The track leads through the farmyard and just over the wall on your right you will see the little church of St Andrew.

A perfectly preserved 12th-century church, it was furnished in oak during the 18th century, with box pews, a singing gallery, a simple screen, pulpit and tester, now all aged to a delicate silver-grey. It was restored by the architect A.R. Powys in the 1920s using the proceeds of a sale of Thomas Hardy's manuscripts and a donation from Lord Esher.

5. Retrace your steps past the farm to the point where you turned left for Winterborne Tomson. Keep ahead for a few yards then turn left through an iron gate.

Winterborne Zelston – *The Botany Bay Inne*

6 Keep straight ahead over the meadow, go through another iron gate and continue with a hedge on your left to Muston Lane.

7 Turn left to see part of Anderson Manor.

With its heavy gables and stone-mullioned windows, the manor has remained almost unaltered for three and a half centuries. During the Second World War it was requisitioned and became the headquarters of the Special Operations Small Raiding Force.

8 Retrace your steps up Muston Lane and follow the lane ahead for about ½ mile to breaks on either side of the hedges marked with blue arrow bridleway signs. (On my last visit the right-hand sign was broken.)

9 Leave Muston Lane and turn right beside a field with a hedge on your right. The path follows the course of a Roman road and leads through gates to a cross-track.

10 Turn left and after just a few yards you leave the Roman road which continues north-east to Badbury Rings and instead turn right through a gate to follow a woodland footpath. The path leads through a gate and bears a little left to a cross-track at Great Coll Wood.

11 Turn right to leave the woods and go through a gate into a field. Down the field a little to your right you will see Bushes Farm. There is no clear path at this point but bear a little right down the field, past a short wooden post on your left, towards some fence posts you will see through a gap in the hedge at the foot of the field. With the fence posts on your left, follow a wide green path passing Bushes Farm on your right and continue down the lane past the church in Winterborne Zelston. Retrace your steps through the village to the Botany Bay Inne.

PLACE OF INTEREST NEARBY

White Mill near Sturminster Marshall dates back to medieval times and has been restored by the National Trust. It is open for guided tours between Easter and October.
✆ 01258 858051; postcode BH21 4BX

Moreton
The Frampton Arms
3 miles (4.8 km)

Moreton is a tiny village of mostly cob or brick cottages, many deep thatched with diamond-paned windows. Set beside the River Frome in Thomas Hardy's 'Vale of Great Dairies', the village seems to have changed little since his day. But Moreton draws visitors from all over the world! They come to admire the church which is stunningly beautiful, lit by a glorious sequence of engraved glass windows, and to visit the grave of one of our greatest heroes, Lawrence of Arabia, who is buried in the nearby churchyard.

After a visit to Lawrence's grave and the church, the route of this walk leads you across the Frome to follow woodland paths Lawrence would have known before returning over the water meadows to Moreton.

THE FRAMPTON ARMS was built in the 1840s to coincide with the opening of the local railway station. The name comes from a local land-

MORETON – *The Frampton Arms*

10

owning family who built it. There is a cosy atmosphere inside and a lovely terrace and enclosed beer garden with children's play equipment outside. On the lunch menu you'll find freshly cooked pub classics, along with sandwiches and salads, all made using locally sourced ingredients. Dinner is a slightly grander affair, but the good-sized menu should suit everyone. Should you wish to stay the night there are 14 nicely furnished rooms.

✆ 01305 852253; postcode DT2 8BB

Alternatively, try the **DOVECOTE CAFE** which you will find towards the back of the car park, near The Walled Garden. Open 7 days a week, there is seating indoors and outside in the pleasant gardens.

> **How to get there:** From the A35, turn for Affpuddle along the B3390. Follow the signs for Moreton and turn left for the village. From the A352 turn for Moreton along the B3390 and shortly after the level crossing turn right for the village.
> **Parking:** In the centre of Moreton. Drive through the village and turn right for East Burton and Wool. Park in the large parking area beside the road on your right.
> **Map:** OS Explorer Outdoor Leisure 15 Purbeck and South Dorset (GR: SY804893).

THE WALK

1 Turn right from the parking area, following the sign for East Burton and Wool. After about 50 yards, go through a white gateway on your right leading into the burial ground. Take the path straight ahead and at the far end is the grave of Lawrence of Arabia.

How did he come to be buried here? In an attempt to escape publicity he had enlisted as a Private in the Tank Corps based at nearby Bovington Camp. His cousins, the Frampton family, owned Moreton Estate. He rented a small cottage, Clouds Hill, from them as a retreat. In 1935, Lawrence died, following an accident on his motorbike in the narrow lanes near Clouds Hill and his family asked their cousins if he could be buried in Moreton. His funeral was attended by many prominent people, including Sir Winston and Lady Churchill.

2 Turn left to retrace your steps and keep straight ahead along the

Pub Walks in Dorset

FOLLOWING THE JUBILEE TRAIL IN MORETON WOODS

'No-Through-Road', following the sign 'To the Church'. Turn right through the white gate leading to the Moreton Estate and follow the drive to the church.

The church was almost completely destroyed by a bomb in 1940. Work on the present sequence of windows began in 1950 from designs by Lawrence Whistler and later windows were engraved solely by the artist. They are based on the theme of light. The Trinity Chapel window is one of the most moving, commemorating a Royal Air Force pilot who was shot down over France.

MORETON – *The Frampton Arms*

③ Return through the white gate and turn right to cross the long bridge spanning the ford over the Frome. Follow the path straight ahead through the trees. The path curves left crossing a branch of the Frome to bring you to a signpost.

④ There are several tracks at this point. Keep ahead following the sign 'Lawrence Trail–Clouds Hill'. Continue through an area now cleared of trees for about ½ mile to a footpath sign on your left by some large boulders.

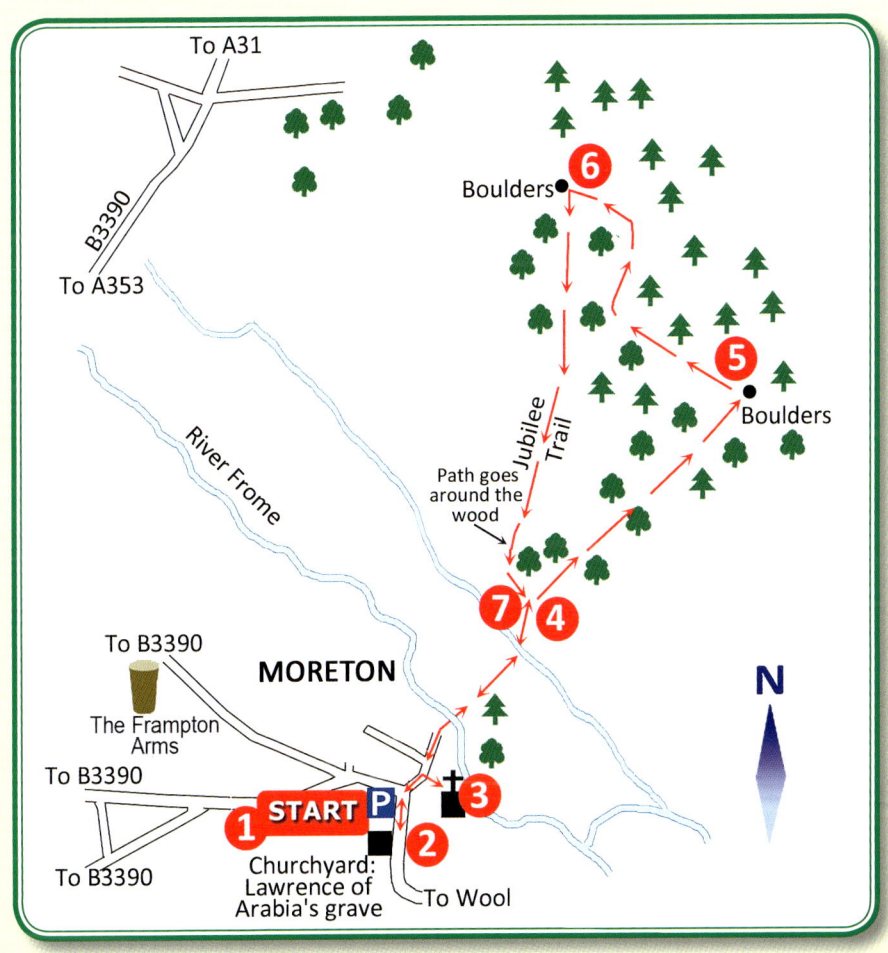

Pub Walks in Dorset

5 Turn left past the boulders and follow the wide path through the trees past a track on the right. Keep to the same path as it weaves its way through the woods and over open ground colourful with wild flowers attracting hordes of butterflies.

6 Now for some careful navigation! When you see some large boulders about 50 yards ahead (like the ones you saw at point 5) look carefully to the left of your track for a post marked with a green and yellow Jubilee Trail sign. Do not go past the boulders but turn left to follow the Jubilee Trail. The path runs through oak woods and over small footbridges. Leave the woods to cross a footbridge. Walk straight over the field ahead and cross another footbridge. Keep straight on over the field. Walk beside the next field with a fence on your left and follow the line of the fence as it curves round the edge of a wood then bears left to a stile. (This differs a little from the OS map which shows the path leading straight on through the wood.)

7 Cross the stile to meet the broad bridleway you followed after crossing the bridge over the Frome. Turn right and at the division turn right again to return over the bridge to Moreton.

PLACES OF INTEREST NEARBY

Clouds Hill, now the property of the National Trust, is a simple brick and tile cottage that became Lawrence of Arabia's retreat from 1923 until his death in 1935. The cottage is as he left it. Telephone for opening times: ☎ 01929 405616; postcode BH20 7NQ

Bovington Tank Museum contains tanks and armoured cars from all parts of the world, many in diorama settings. There is a café and gift shop. ☎ 01929 405096; postcode BH20 6JG

Monkey World is home to chimpanzees, Orang Utans and Barbary apes. Many other animals enjoy their freedom in large heathland enclosures. There is a pets corner and an adventure trail, plus a restaurant and gift shop. Open daily from 10am to 5pm.
☎ 01929 462537; postcode BH20 6HH

Winterborne Stickland
The Crown Inn
4½ miles (7.2 km)

Winterborne Stickland is hidden away in a quiet valley in the chalk downs, East of Blandford Forum. It is a real 'working' village with everything a village should have: attractive houses, an interesting church, a school, an excellent shop and post office and a welcoming pub. If you add beautiful scenery to this list, you have the perfect starting point for a walk!

Meadow paths lead you east over the Winterborne stream to take a woodland path winding up the down. After an exhilarating walk high on the downs, you follow a wide valley to explore the countryside west of the village. This remote area is exceptionally rich in wildlife.

Pub Walks in Dorset

The **CROWN INN**, its colour-washed walls gleaming beneath a roof of dark thatch, dates back to the 17th century. Inside, the pub seems to have changed little since then, with its huge inglenook fireplace and heavily-beamed ceilings. You'll find friendly staff and a good menu which includes plenty of pub favourites along with delicious pizzas.
✆ 01258 881042; postcode DT11 0NJ

> **How to get there:** The best approach is via the A354. Turn for Winterborne Stickland in Winterborne Whitechurch and follow the lane for about 3 miles to the village.
> **Parking:** The Crown car park.
> **Map:** OS Explorer 117 Cerne Abbas and Bere Regis (GR: ST837047).

THE WALK

① The walk begins beside the main road through the village opposite the Crown Inn. Pass the front of the inn on your right and continue for about 150 yards to a bridleway on your left signed for Winterborne Houghton.

② Turn left and follow the path as it climbs between hedges and go through a gate. Take the narrow path ahead which runs half-left over a meadow. The path meets a hedge and curves right with the hedge on the left.

③ After about 100 yards turn left through a small iron gate in the hedge. Follow the path running steeply downhill, cross a bridge over the Winterborne stream and descend the steps leading to a lane.

④ Turn right beside the lane for about 100 yards. Then take the bridleway on the left to go through a gate. Follow the path ahead which winds uphill through woods to a lane.

⑤ Turn right and in a few yards turn left to follow the bridleway past Valley View Farm and go through a gate. Follow the gravel track ahead past some farm buildings.

⑥ Ignore a gate on your right and go through the gate immediately ahead

Winterborne Stickland – *The Crown Inn*

into a meadow. Bear half-right diagonally down the meadow, then climb up to the point in the far corner where three hedges converge.

7 Go through a gate and walk up the meadow ahead with a hedge on your right. Through the next gate you reach a cross-path.

8 Turn left and follow the grassy path beside fields with a thick hedge on your left. You are now high on the downs with wide views eastwards towards the Stour valley. After about ¾ mile the path descends into the Winterborne valley. Go through a gate and keep ahead beside a meadow. Through the next gate a small wooden bridge over the stream brings you to the road.

9 Cross straight over the road, go through a gate and follow the grassy track ahead up the valley. Shortly you have a wire fence on your left. After about ¼ mile turn left through a gate and walk up the field ahead with the fence on your left. At the top of the field turn right, still with the fence on your left. Soon the fence gives way to more thick hedges,

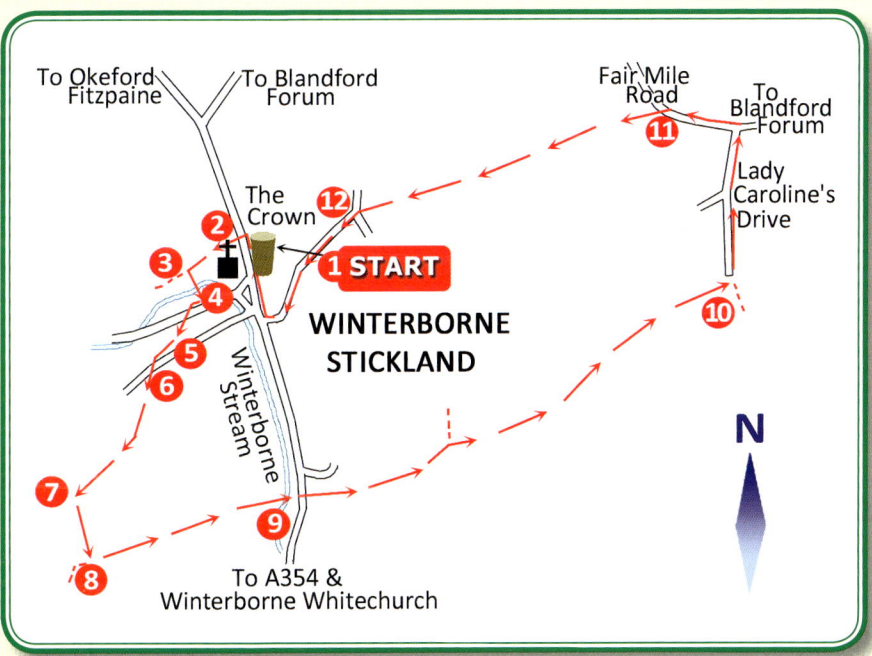

57

Pub Walks in Dorset

alive with yellowhammers, goldfinches and blackcaps. Follow the grassy track over the downs for a mile to go under power cables to a gate opening to a broad track.

10 Turn left to follow the track with a hedge on your right and a fence on your left. This is known as Lady Caroline's Drive.

I am grateful to Deidre Sprackling in Winterborne Stickland post office for explaining the reason for the name. Baron Hambro, the Danish banker, bought a huge estate including the village of Winterborne Stickland in 1852. Lady Caroline Hambro would be driven along this route on her way to Blandford Forum. The village remained in the Hambro family, who provided the village school and the village hall. When Lord Hambro gave the land for the hall to the village, he stipulated it must always be called 'The Pamela Hambro Hall' in memory of his wife who tragically drowned in a boating accident.

Cross the top of a lane and keep ahead past a gate to Fair Mile Road. Turn left and after about 200 yards you will reach a point where the road starts to curve right.

11 Turn left off the bend here through a gate. Follow the fieldside path heading west, with a hedge on your right, for over a mile to cross a gated lane.

12 Continue downhill to the road in the valley and turn right to walk through Winterborne Stickland towards the church. In front of the church gates, sheltered by a lime tree, are the remains of a medieval preaching cross. The church dates from the 13th century. The nave and part of the chancel have fine 16th-century wagon roofs and a 15th-century sculpture of the Holy Rood has been built into the wall of the porch.

PLACE OF INTEREST NEARBY

Blandford Forum is an elegant Georgian market town and a visit to the museum illustrates the area's life and culture. Opening times vary so check the website before visiting.
✆ 01258 451115; postcode DT11 7HQ

12

Shillingstone
The Old Ox Inn
4 miles (6.4 km)

Shillingstone lies beside the River Stour at the foot of one of Dorset's mightiest hill forts, Hambledon Hill. And if you are a railway enthusiast, a visit to Shillingstone is a must! Shillingstone Station opened in 1863 and is the last surviving village station on the route of the former Somerset and Dorset Railway from Bournemouth to Bath.

Although the route follows footpaths through the gently undulating countryside of this quiet corner of the Blackmore Vale and reaches no great height, you enjoy magnificent views over the wooded slopes of the downs.

The **OLD OX INN** is a traditional family-run pub. Welcoming and comfortable, it is the centre of village life. Walkers are regular visitors, as

Pub Walks in Dorset

you might expect being located at the foot of Hambledon Hill, and all are well catered for. All the food is homemade and the menu includes light bites as well as heartier steaks, burgers and plenty of pub classics. The owner told me that, unsurprisingly, the village is steam mad and sometimes 'steam ups' are held in the pub grounds!

✆ 01258 860055; postcode DT11 0SF

> **How to get there:** Shillingstone is beside the A357 between Sturminster Newton and Blandford Forum. The walk starts from the Old Ox Inn which faces the road near the southern end of the village.
> **Parking:** The inn car park.
> **Map:** OS Landranger 194 Dorchester and Weymouth shows the whole route on one map (GR: ST827109).

THE WALK

1. Cross the road in front of the Old Ox Inn and turn left to walk through the village, with the road on your left.

2. At this point the pavement ceases. Cross the road and take Holloway Lane signed for the Trailway. Continue along the lane under the arch of the former railway, following the sign for Hanford. Pass a track on your left leading into Alders Copse and go through a gate into a field.

3. Bear a little right over the field and cross a gated bridge over the Stour.

4. Turn left to walk beside the river towards a belt of woodland. As you approach the woods bear slightly right through a gateway. Keep ahead for only about 50 yards, then go through a small wooden gate on your left to a narrow footpath leading through the trees.

5. When the path finishes, turn right through a gate and continue beside a field with a hedge on the left. Go through a gate and keep ahead over the gravel passing all the farm buildings on your right with hedges on your left. Go through a gate and follow a grassy fenced track leading through double gates to a lane in Hanford. Across the lane you will see Jacobean Hanford Manor, now a preparatory school.

Shillingstone – *The Old Ox Inn*

12

6. Turn left along the lane which curves right to meet the Child Okeford road.

7. Turn left to follow the road for about ½ mile.

8. Turn left up an unsigned lane (first on your left) towards some houses. After about 200 yards, turn right following a bridleway sign past a farm building on your right.

9. Navigate carefully here! Continue for only about 40 yards, then ignore the gate immediately ahead and **turn left** down a partly gravelled track with a hedge on your left and a fence on your right. The track leads downhill, then turns right

Shillingstone station is the last surviving village station on the former Somerset and Dorset line from Bournemouth to Bath

61

Pub Walks in Dorset

before curving round a belt of trees to lead up to a cross-track by a farm building.

10 Turn left down a grassy track leaving the building on your right.

11 At this point, navigate carefully again as the right-of-way did not follow the OS map. When the track curves left, keep ahead for only a few yards and look for a narrow path on your right leading through the hedge to a small wooden gate. (It is just before the track curves right to a ruined barn.) The right-of-way continues straight over the field ahead to a gate leading to a hedged track but if the field is planted you may prefer to walk round the field to the gate.

12 Cross the track, climb the stile and bearing very slightly left (misleading yellow arrow) walk down the field and cross the bridge over the Stour. Bear left along a clear path leading to the Trailway.

13 The shorter route crosses the Trailway and follows the path ahead for Shillingstone village. If you wish to visit the station, turn right along the Trailway.

As you approach the station, turn left over the crossing and bear right along the footpath to the station buildings.

Under the auspices of the North Dorset Railway Trust, the Shillingstone Railway project aims to restore part of the track with points and build a lifestyle museum with working steam locomotives.

After your visit, retrace your steps and turn right to rejoin the shorter route. When you come to a lane turn right and after a few yards, take the footpath on the left for the Blandford road. Bear right to a lane which turns left to the road. Turn left to walk down the village to the Old Ox Inn.

PLACE OF INTEREST NEARBY

Shillingstone station is open Wednesday, Saturday and Sunday from 10am to 4pm and other days as shown on its website. There is on-site parking, a café and a shop. Entry is free.
✆ 01258 860696; postcode DT11 0SA

Hinton St Mary
The White Horse Inn
5½ miles (8.8 km)

Hinton St Mary is an enchanting village built of pale gold stone standing on a ridge overlooking the Blackmore Vale. Once a great forest, the Vale is now a patchwork of low grassy hills and small thickly hedged fields. Winding steep banked lanes lead to villages and farms surrounded by lush pastures. Thomas Hardy describes the scenery in *Tess of the d'Urbervilles* and in some of his finest poetry. But the Vale is also known as the home of Dorset's other much-loved poet, William Barnes. This is a walk in the footsteps of both poets.

From Hinton St Mary, footpaths lead you down to the Stour and along the valley to Sturminster Newton passing Riverside Villa where Hardy spent two happy years with his first wife Emma. After heading west to cross the Stour, the route heads north to the parish of Bagber, where Barnes was born in 1801, and follows him over the fields to Cutt Mill where he played as a boy. Field paths take you back to Hinton St Mary.

Pub Walks in Dorset

The **WHITE HORSE INN** is a friendly family-run traditional village inn with attractive décor, low ceilings, deep window seats and huge old-fashioned fireplaces. The real ales are seasonally rotated and all the food is home cooked and superb. The menu offers a tempting array of bar snacks and well-presented main courses, and it's worth leaving enough room for one of the delicious desserts. We also found the staff to be very welcoming and attentive, making this a destination in itself so definitely worth a visit.
✆ 01258 472723; postcode DT10 1NA

> **How to get there:** Hinton St Mary is beside the B3092 a mile north of Sturminster Newton. Approaching from Sturminster, drive into the village and take the first road on the right which leads up to the Inn. Approaching from the north drive into the village and take the second road on the left.
> **Parking:** The White Horse Inn car park.
> **Map:** OS Explorer 129 Yeovil and Sherborne (GR: ST787142).

THE WALK

1 Turn right from the front door of the White Horse, cross the B3092 and continue down Wood Lane to a footpath sign on the left for Sturminster Newton and Mill.

2 Turn left along the track and when it divides, bear left to walk downhill round the edge of a field with trees close on your left.

3 After about ½ mile, look carefully for a narrow signed path going through the trees on your left. The path leads through a gate to the hillside above the Stour and climbs up to the top of the ridge crowned by the houses of Sturminster Newton. The path traces the ridge then drops downhill to lead through a gate and follow the river valley. Continue under the arch of the former railway viaduct and keep straight on over all cross-tracks. The path rises to a small gate. On the corner you will see two semi-detached Victorian villas. The first house is Riverside Villa where Hardy brought Emma in 1876.

4 Retrace your steps down the hill and keep ahead to the first cross-path.

Hinton St Mary – *The White Horse Inn* 🔴13

CUTT MILL

5. Here you leave the path to Hinton St Mary. Turn left and after a few yards you will see the white railings of Colber Bridge.

6. Cross the bridge and in order to avoid a possible bull, take the left-hand path signed 'Stalbridge Lane and Road Lane Farm'. Continue over the meadow, go through a small gate and follow the narrow hedged path to Stalbridge Lane.

7. Turn right along the lane following the sign 'Bagber via Stalbridge

Pub Walks in Dorset

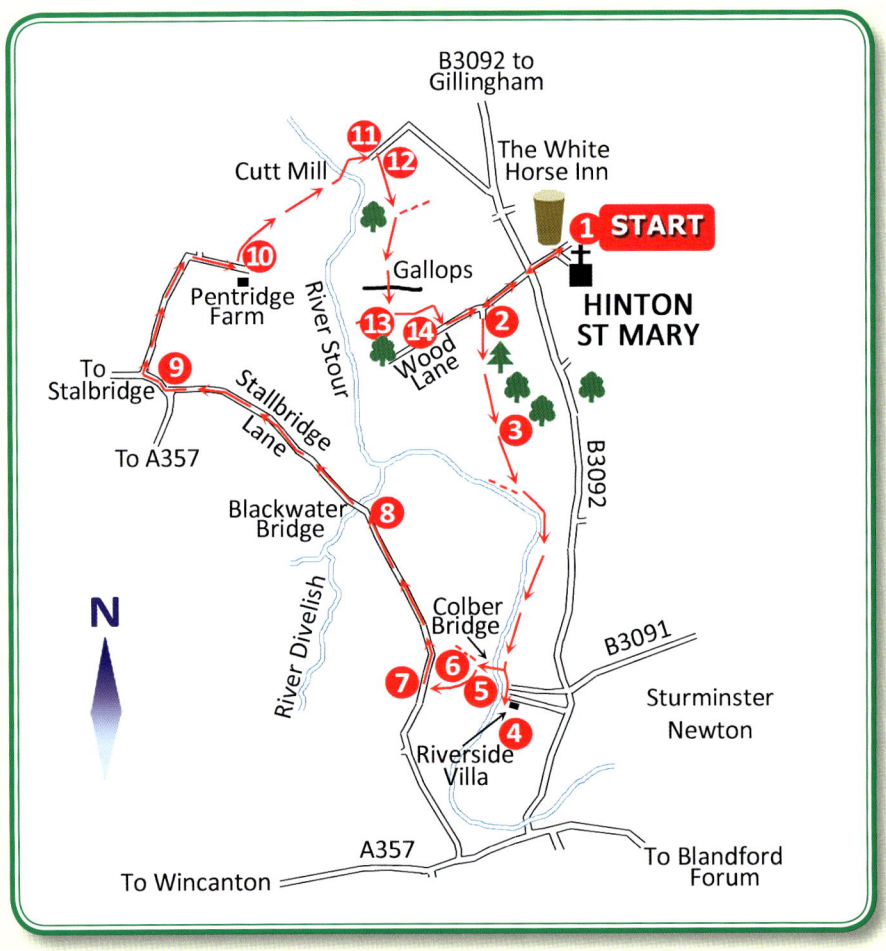

Lane'. Keep ahead over a cross-track. The lane becomes a track to Blackwater Bridge over the River Divelish, a tributary of the Stour.

8 Cross the bridge and follow the narrow footpath ahead. The path broadens to become a tree-bordered track leading to a minor road by Manor Farm.

9 Turn right along the road for about 150 yards, then turn right again along an unsigned lane. Pass Bagber House Farm on the left and

Hinton St Mary – *The White Horse Inn*

continue over the bridge of the disused railway. The lane swings right past Lower Bagber Farm. You will see a bridleway sign on your right pointing left. That is our way but if you continue past the sign for a few yards you will glimpse Pentridge Farm, once the home of Barnes' uncle and aunt. He recalls many happy hours with them in his poem *A Rustic Childood*.

10 Turn left following the sign through a rusty iron gate and keep ahead past a house on the left and a barn on the right. Continue through gates down the meadows to Cutt Mill. The pond and weir are still impressive but sadly the mill is now in ruins. Cross the bridge and walk past the mill to a road.

11 Bear right uphill. Pass a stile and footpath sign for Sturminster Newton on your right. Continue uphill for a few more yards to a bridleway on your right signed for Wood Lane.

12 Turn right and follow the path through woods. The path becomes a wide track which shortly curves left uphill. Leave the track and keep straight ahead. When the path leaves the woods, continue beside a field with trees on the right. Cross the open hillside and keep ahead over a railed gallop. Follow the path over the field ahead to a wide grassy cross-path.

13 There is no sign but turn left up the field. After about 150 yards, turn right to follow a bridleway to Wood Lane.

14 Turn left to walk up to the B3092. Cross over and walk up the road ahead to return to the White Horse Inn.

PLACE OF INTEREST NEARBY

Sturminster Newton Mill is a working water mill dating from the 17th century. The mill is open from Easter to the end of September, weekends, Monday and Thursday from 11am to 5pm.
✆ 01747 854 355; postcode DT10 1AN

Evershot
The Acorn Inn
4 miles (6.4 km)

This route runs almost entirely through the parkland surrounding Melbury House. It is in open landscape of green hills and valley, with magnificent plantations of trees. The park and the fine house it surrounds were acquired in 1500 by Henry Strangways. His son, Sir Giles, rebuilt and extended the property and in the 18th century part of the building was remodelled in the classic style. Today the Strangways family still own Melbury House.

The walk begins in Evershot, close to the southern gate of the park, and follows paths and lanes to give a fine view of Melbury House. We return through the Deer Park. Red deer predominate but you may also spot fallow, sika and Père David's deer, a rare Chinese species.

EVERSHOT – *The Acorn Inn*

14

The **ACORN INN**, immortalised by Thomas Hardy as 'The Sow-and-Acorn' in his novel *Tess of the d'Urbervilles*, is a mellow stone-built inn and one of Dorset's most delightful hostelries. Here you will receive a warm welcome and enjoy the peaceful atmosphere of a traditional country inn with an award-winning restaurant. Inside you'll find attractive décor with soft lighting, oak panelling and roaring fires. Outside there is a pleasant spacious beer garden ideal for warmer days.

Ingredients are locally and sustainably sourced, with herbs grown in the pub's own garden. There is a wide range of local ales available and a choice of well-selected wines.

Excellent accommodation is provided in rooms named after locations from Thomas Hardy's books.

✆ 01935 83228; postcode DT2 0JW

How to get there: Evershot is a small village midway between Yeovil and Dorchester. Approach via the A37, take the turning for Evershot and continue for about 1½ miles to the Acorn Inn on your right.
Parking: The inn car park.
Map: OS Explorer 117 Cerne Abbas and Bere Regis (GR: ST582079).

THE WALK

1 Turn left from the entrance to the inn to walk through the village. No two houses are alike in Evershot. Some reflect the 17th century with their mullioned windows and arched doorways, others are small and thatched.

2 When the main road curves right keep straight on, passing a stone seat beneath a large tree on your right, and follow the lane up the private drive – footpath only – into Melbury Park.

3 After about 150 yards take the joining lane on the right leading uphill. The lane becomes a gravel track and emerges from the trees at the top of the hill to reveal a fine view over the valley to the wooded slopes of Bubb Down Hill. Follow the track downhill over all crosstracks to a crossing track at the foot of the hillside.

Pub Walks in Dorset

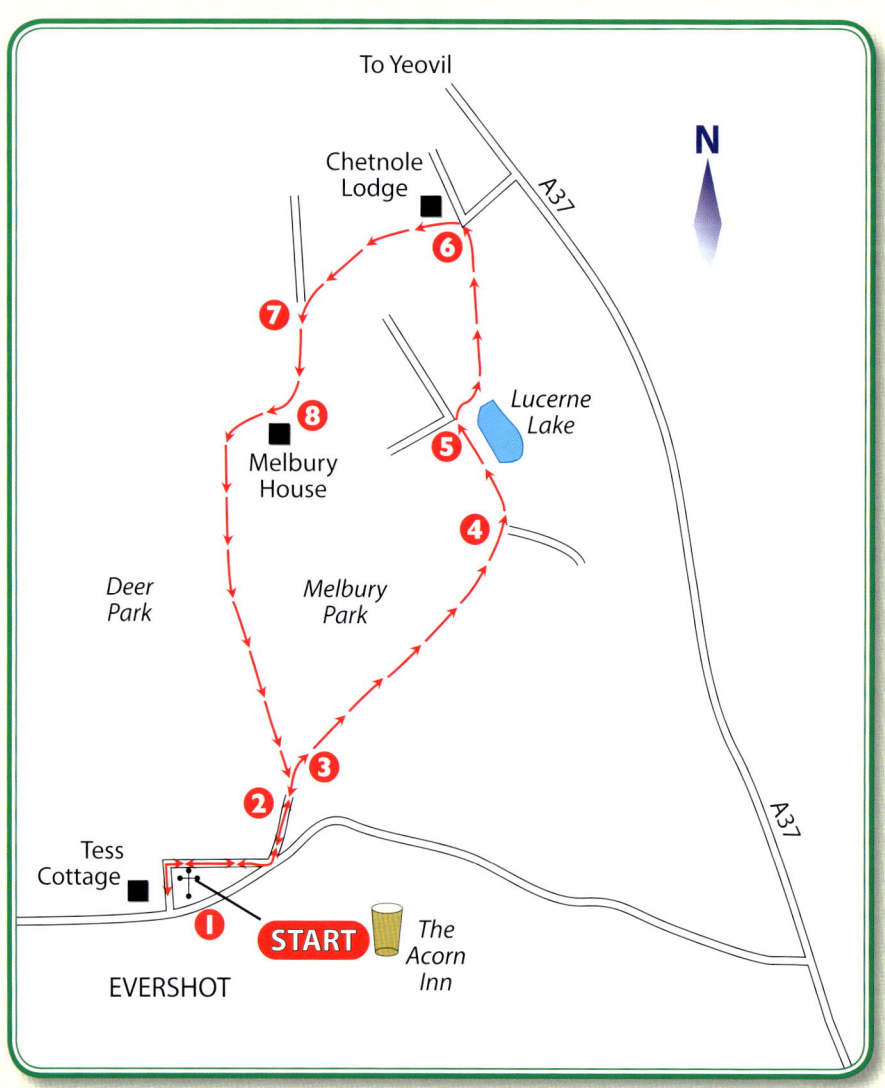

④ Turn left following the sign for 'Mel Osm.' (Melbury Osmond). On your right you will catch glimpses of Lucerne Lake and as you near the northern end of the lake you have a better view of the water with a thatched boathouse beside it. The track begins to curve right.

Evershot – *The Acorn Inn*

5. Leave the main track here (which continues uphill) and turn sharp right round the head of the lake. (Look for a bridleway sign just round the corner.) Continue over a bridge and keep ahead beside a field with a fence on your right to go through a small gate in the far corner. Bear left beneath the trees to meet a tarmac lane.

6. Turn left, leaving Chetnole Lodge on your right, to walk through the park. Continue past a cottage on your left to follow the lane to a T-junction.

7. Turn left toward the impressive north front of Melbury House. Thomas Hardy set many of the scenes in the first edition of his novel The Woodlanders in this area. He called the great house 'King's Hintock Court'. Giles Winterborne, an evicted villager, is forced to make his home in 'One-Chimney Hut' in the woods nearby.

8. The lane swings right through gates to cross the Deer Park. Continue along the lane to leave Melbury Park and rejoin our outward-bound route at point 3. Retrace your steps past the seat and tree and after a few yards turn right to follow Back Lane, which finally curves left. The lane meets the main road between the church on your left and the cottage where Hardy's Tess stopped for breakfast on your right. Turn left to return to the Acorn.

PLACE OF INTEREST NEARBY

The small church at nearby Melbury Bubb, reached via Chetnole, is well worth a visit. Still lit by oil lamps, it has a beaker-shaped Saxon font with upside down carvings of a dragon and hounds chasing deer and some beautiful 15th-century stained glass.

St Mary's Church, Melbury Bubb

Cerne Abbas
The New Inn
2¾ miles (4.2 km)

Our walk passes the ruins of the Benedictine abbey founded in 987 and climbs Giant Hill giving splendid views over the Cerne valley. A gentle descent down the opposite side of the hill brings you back to the village.

Find time to explore Cerne Abbas. A historic and beautiful village, it lies cradled in the downs where a little stream finishes its journey south and meets the Cerne. The chalk outline of its famous giant dominates the village from a westward-facing hillside. No two of the fascinating houses lining its narrow streets are alike. Some, half- timbered, project upper storeys over your head, others are stone-built and banded with flint while others reflect the grace of Georgian days with rounded bow windows and pedimented doorways.

Cerne Abbas – *The New Inn*

The **NEW INN** is a stone-built hostelry that has welcomed walkers since the 13th century when it served as a dormitory for the abbey, offering rest and refreshment for passing pilgrims. In the mid-16th century it became Cerne's principal coaching inn. Today the inn continues to offer a warm welcome, well-appointed accommodation and excellent food and drink. The bar areas are spacious and comfortable and there is a separate restaurant. The menu both in the bar and restaurant offers a wide selection of interesting and varied dishes, which includes sandwiches, pub classics and a traditional cream tea. Behind the inn you will find a patio and a beautiful walled garden. If you fancy a longer stay the New Inn offers excellent accommodation.

✆ 01300 341274; postcode DT2 7JF

> **How to get there:** Cerne Abbas is about 5 miles north of Dorchester signed off the A352. The walk begins from the public car park and picnic place. Turn off the A352 down the lane signed 'picnic place' leaving the viewing area for the Cerne Abbas Giant directly on your left. After about 50 yards turn left and park.
> **Parking:** Kettle Bridge Car Park.
> **Map:** OS Explorer 117 Cerne Abbas and Bere Regis (GR: ST663014).

THE WALK

1. Turn left from the entrance to the picnic area to walk down to a stream. Turn right before the bridge and follow the streamside to a bridge on the left. Cross this and follow the path to Abbey Street. Facing the street, on your left is Abbey Farm and the entrance to the abbey ruins.

2. With the entrance to the ruins on your left go through an iron gate into the churchyard. Take the left-hand of the two paths ahead to leave the churchyard through another gate. Bear half-right up the meadow which is ridged with embankments. When you reach a dip in the highest embankment and the trees are close on your left, look carefully for a kissing gate a little uphill on the left.

3. Go through the kissing gate and turn left along the foot of Giant Hill. When the path divides take the right-hand path uphill which bears left to the open hillside. Go past the area around the giant to climb

Pub Walks in Dorset

the hillside. The soft turf is starred with wild flowers and alive with butterflies in summer.

4. At the top cross a stile into a field. Keep ahead over the field following the waymarker and sign for the Wessex Ridgeway.

5. When you reach a four-way signpost walk straight ahead across a field following the Cerne Valley Trail waymarker and making for a large bush at the far side (there may be no clear path).

6. Go through a gate and turn right along the crest of the hill. Below you Cerne Abbas nestles in the valley.

7. After about 100 yards you come to a signpost. Navigate carefully here! Ignore the obvious track leading ahead and bear a little left to follow a path downhill towards Cerne Abbas. When you are nearly in the valley the path divides and a narrow path leads right to continue round the foot of Giant Hill. Continue past this turning for about 30 yards and look carefully for another narrow path on the right leading to a stile.

8. Turn right over the stile and bear half-left down the meadow to cross a stile on the corner of a sports field. Keep ahead, with a fence to the left,

HALF-TIMBERED HOUSES IN CERNE ABBAS VILLAGE

Cerne Abbas – *The New Inn*

15

then turn right along the foot of the meadow to go through a gate on your left to a lane. Turn right into Cerne Abbas. Keep straight on to the New Inn on your left.

To return to your car turn right from the entrance to the New Inn. Turn left up Abbey Street past the church on your right. Note the stocks! Turn left again before Abbey Farm and retrace your steps to the picnic area.

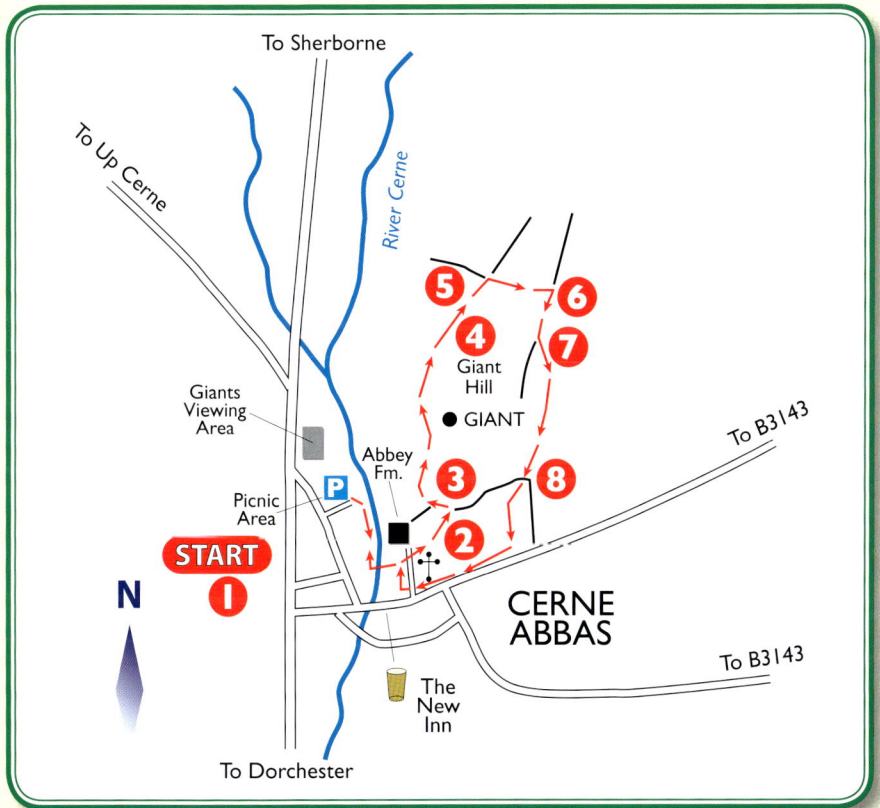

PLACE OF INTEREST NEARBY

The **Guest House and Porch** to the Abbot's lodging can be visited for a small fee.

Cattistock
The Fox & Hounds
4½ miles (7.2 km)

Cattistock is a picturesque village in the valley of the River Frome, 8 miles north-west of Dorchester. The pub, where you start this walk, faces a small square which is surrounded by houses with thatched roofs and gleaming white stone walls. Dominating the square is the great tower of the Church of St Peter and St Paul. The village is surrounded by glorious countryside. A network of quiet leafy lanes and tracks provide an easy way to explore this remote area of the downs.

Cattistock – *The Fox & Hounds*

16

The route leads north from the village then crosses the Frome to head west along the valley of one of the river's tributaries to Lower Wraxall. This stream-side hamlet is rural Dorset at its most enchanting. You return along a track which follows the other side of the valley and rises to give beautiful downland views. Before crossing the river, the route leads through Chilfrome, an attractive village set among woodland, fields and orchards. You return to the pub along a footpath leading past Cattistock church.

The **FOX & HOUNDS** is a 16th-century inn that has been skilfully renovated and retains many old world features, including huge inglenook fireplaces, stone mullioned windows and heavily beamed ceilings. The pub is deservedly popular and a favourite with the crew of HMS *Cattistock* whose flag hangs in the church. Palmer's Dorset Gold, Best Bitter and Copper Ale are on offer. All the food is homemade and produced locally, if possible. Accommodation is available.
✆ 01300 320444; postcode DT2 0JH

> **How to get there:** Approach via the A356 and Maiden Newton, or turn for Cattistock off the A37.
> **Parking:** The inn car park.
> **Map:** OS Explorer 117 Cerne Abbas and Bere Regis (GR: SY592998).

THE WALK

1 Leave the front of the Fox & Hounds and turn right. The Savill Memorial Hall is on your left. It is named in memory of Frank Savill of Chantmarle who died from his wounds in 1916 during the First World War. Chantmarle is a large Jacobean mansion north of the village and the hall is built in the same style. Follow the lane as it curves right then curves right again to lead slightly uphill through the village. You will see an iron village pump on the left before you come to the shop.

2 Keep ahead past the turning on the right for Chalmington following the sign for Wraxall. The lane crosses a bridge over the former Somerset and Dorset railway then drops to take you over the Frome, just a small stream at this point. Here it is joined by a tributary flowing south through Lower Wraxall.

Pub Walks in Dorset

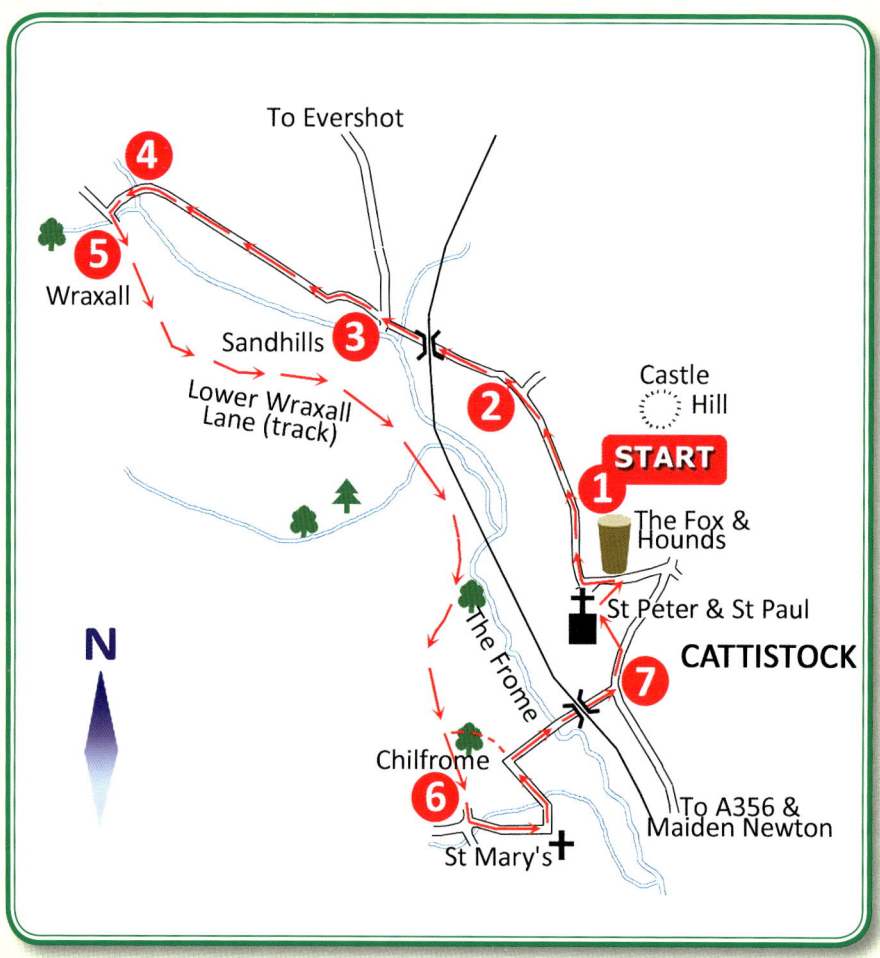

3. Pass the turning on the right for Evershot and follow the lane ahead, bordered by high hedges and banks of wild flowers. Occasionally the hedges part to reveal views of the meadows sloping down to the stream with the wooded hillsides beyond.

4. The lane curves left downhill to cross the stream into Lower Wraxall then turns sharply right uphill. Leave the lane and turn left past a long thatched house on your right and cross the small footbridge over a stream.

Cattistock – *The Fox & Hounds*

16

THE FOOTPATH TO CATTISTOCK CHURCH

5. Follow the track ahead which rises gently uphill then winds along the western side of the valley. When the tributary meets the Frome, it continues south along the hillside bordering the river past a track on the left. The track descends closer to the river and can be muddy for about 100 yards before rising and becoming dry again underfoot. A

Pub Walks in Dorset

short climb brings you past Grove Stall Farm and you are rewarded by a magnificent view over the Frome valley. The surface of the track becomes metalled as it leads steeply downhill cutting a deep tunnel between tree roots and banks of ferns into Chilfrome village.

6 At the crossroads in the village turn left following the sign for Cattistock. Opposite St Mary's church on the right, the lane curves left again signed 'Frome Valley Trail'. The lane swings right to cross the Frome, run under a railway bridge and meet the road approaching Cattistock.

7 Turn left for about 100 yards, then turn left through a small iron gate and follow the footpath ahead towards the church of St Peter and St Paul.

The church was rebuilt in the 19th century by the architect Sir George Gilbert Scott. The north aisle and the tower, which until a disastrous fire in 1940 housed a carillon of 33 bells, were the work of his son. This magnificent church has been called 'the Cathedral of the Frome Valley'.

Keep ahead beside a wall to walk through the churchyard. Beside the path in a hollow on your left you will see what I believe to be an old healing well. Stone steps lead down to a basin filled with water from a spring which I am told never runs dry. The stone above the basin is carved with a crucifix. Leave the churchyard through the gates on your right and walk down to the square opposite the Fox & Hounds.

PLACE OF INTEREST NEARBY

The Kingcombe Centre is situated in idyllic surroundings beside the river Hooke, west of the A356, about four miles west of Cattistock. The land is farmed in the traditional way avoiding pesticides and herbicides. Courses are run on a variety of subjects and visitors can enjoy the abundance of wildflowers and wildlife. Accommodation is available on a bed and breakfast basis for long or short stays. The café is open every weekend and most days from 1st October to Easter, 11.30am to 3.30pm and from Easter to 30th September, 11.30am to 5pm. ✆ 01300 320684; postcode DT2 0EQ

Abbotsbury
The Swan Inn
4½ miles (7.2 km)

You will enjoy spectacular sea views as you follow the route of this walk from Abbotsbury, one of Dorset's most beautiful villages. The houses and cottages are built of golden stone and many date from the 16th century, with wooden casement windows and reed-thatched roofs. The village is set snugly in a hollow of the coastal downs at the western end of the Fleet, an 8-mile-long tidal lagoon. Benedictine monks founded an abbey here in the 11th century and among the remains of the abbey are a massive tithe barn and the Chapel of St Catherine on the top of Chapel Hill. Abbotsbury's famous Swannery was established by the monks on the shores of the Fleet, an ideal situation protected from prevailing south-westerly gales by the Chesil Bank.

From the village you follow a lane heading south past the Swannery entrance then take the Coast Path which climbs the seaward facing down

Pub Walks in Dorset

to give wonderful views over the Fleet and the Chesil Bank. As you head east along the crest of the down there are more splendid views over the coast, with Portland a dark shadow on the horizon. The return route leaves the coast path to take you inland and follow a hillside footpath back to Abbotsbury.

The landlord of the **SWAN INN** has run his pub for over 50 years and knows exactly how to look after his guests! On a cold day in early spring, I found a friendly welcome, a warm fire, very comfortable seats, home-cooked food and excellent ales. The pub has a spacious beer garden with a lovely countryside view as well as a skittle alley available for private hire. The menu includes tradition pub fayre along with sandwiches and light bites so makes a good post-walk stop.
✆ 01305 871249; postcode DT3 4JL

> **How to get there:** Abbotsbury lies beside the B3157 coastal road about 8 miles west of Weymouth. Approaching from the east the Swan Inn is on your left just before you reach the village. Approaching from the west, drive through the village to the inn which is on your right.
> **Parking:** The Swan Inn car park opposite the inn.
> **Map:** OS Outdoor Leisure 15 Purbeck and South Dorset (GR: SY581852).

THE WALK

1 Turn left from the front door of the Swan to walk into Abbotsbury. When you come to a T-junction turn left following the sign for the Swannery. After a few yards you pass the church of St Nicholas on your left.

The church dates from the 15th century and possesses a panelled Jacobean pulpit with a high back. In the pulpit's canopy are two bullet holes made by Cromwell's men during the Civil War when the church and the nearby manor were held for the King with disastrous consequences.

The road runs downhill and curves right to pass a lake and the huge tithe barn on the left. On top of the hill on your right you will see St Catherine's chapel.

Abbotsbury – *The Swan Inn*

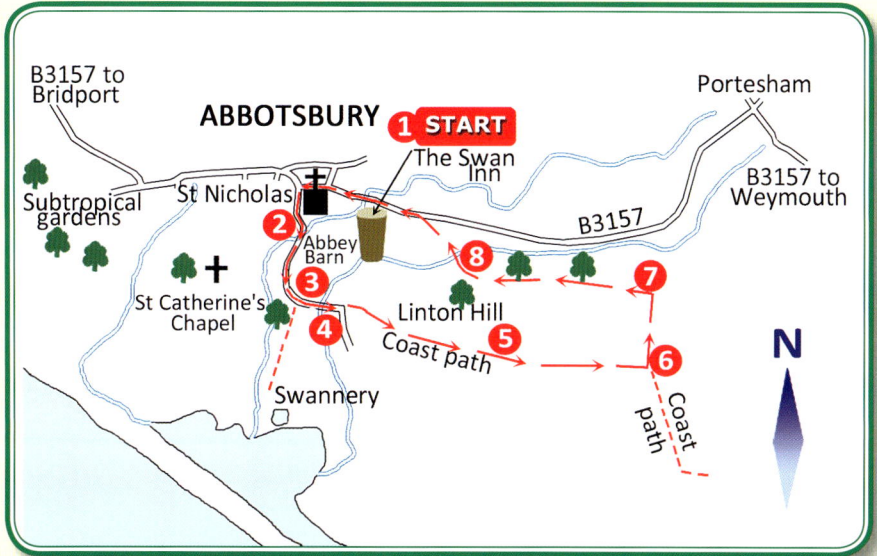

2 As the road rises, turn right down a narrow lane signed as a pedestrian route for the Swannery. The lane leads past the Mill House then curves left past the entrance to the Swannery. Keep ahead to rejoin the road.

3 Turn right along the road towards some farm buildings and pass them on your right.

4 As the road curves right, climb the steps straight ahead and cross a stile to take the Coast Path. Follow the path up the side of a field with a hedge on your left and cross another stone stile. Look back for your first view over the Fleet. A narrow path leads round to the right then winds up the side of Linton Hill. The route is indicated with marker posts. As the path levels, cross a stile and enjoy a splendid walk along the top of the down with stunning views.

5 Pass a footpath on your left, cross a stile and continue along the Coast Path. Go over a farm track and keep ahead with a fence on your right to cross a stone stile. After crossing the next stile a little further on the path drops slightly downhill then continues over a stile to a wide grassy area in front of a stone stile. At this point, you leave the Coast Path which continues over the stone stile then swings right steeply downhill.

Pub Walks in Dorset

6. Turn left to leave the stone stile on your right to go through a large iron farm gate which you will see ahead marked with a yellow arrow footpath sign. Follow the hedged grassy path leading inland. The path drops downhill through a gate to meet a track.

7. Turn left along the track heading west through another gate. You will see St Catherine's Chapel on the hilltop ahead. If the path is obscured by long grass, keep straight on along the hillside aiming for the chapel. Go through a small gate and keep ahead with a hedge on your right. After the next gate you will see Abbotsbury tucked in the valley ahead. Continue along the narrow path along the hillside to go through a gate and keep ahead.

ABBEY RUINS NEAR THE CHURCH

8. Go through the gate and turn right and follow the broad track which winds gently uphill to lead through a gate to the coast road. Turn left to walk beside the road then follow the pavement back to the Swan.

PLACE OF INTEREST NEARBY

At **Abbotsbury Swannery**, in May and June, hundreds of cygnets hatch around the pathways. The Swannery is open all week from March to October from 10am to 5 or 6pm; last admission one hour before closing. Café. You can buy a 'passport' ticket which gives you entry, at a cheaper rate, to the Swannery, the Children's Farm housed in the Tithe Barn and the Subtropical Gardens which are just off the Bridport Road. ✆ 01300 320684; postcode DT3 4JG.

LODERS
The Loders Arms
4½ miles (7.2 km)

Loders lies in a wide green valley beside the River Asker in the West Dorset Hills. Built of honey-gold stone, it is another of Dorset's most attractive villages. Many of the houses are neatly thatched and date from the 17th and 18th centuries. The church, surrounded by the beautiful gardens of a georgian manor house, contains many treasures, including a rare Easter Sepulchre. Not far from the church is the Loders Arms where this walk begins.

From the pub you follow a sunken lane bordered by ferns. You leave the lane to take a bridleway which runs along the valley beside the embankment of the dismantled Bridport to Maiden Newton branch line. The bridleway rises gradually uphill to give far-ranging views over the Loders valley and the surrounding hills. Away to the west on a clear day, you may glimpse Thorncombe Beacon. A hilltop path leads you past the grounds of Mappercombe Manor before you descend into the valley and follow the river to return to the Inn.

Pub Walks in Dorset

The **LODERS ARMS** is a gem of a pub, with a country-wide reputation for excellent food and ales. There is a cosy, heavily beamed bar and a separate, attractively decorated, dining room. And you can be assured of a warm welcome however busy it is. All Palmers ales are on tap. There is a simple but excellent menu which changes regularly and uses local and seasonal produce. Lunch is only available at weekends.
✆ 01308 422431; postcode DT6 3SA

> **How to get there:** Loders is about 5 miles north-east of Bridport. Turn for the village off the A3066 Bridport–Beaminster road or, if approaching via the A35, take the turning heading north for Loders then turn left along the valley to the Loders Arms.
> **Parking:** The Loders Arms car park.
> **Map:** OS Outdoor Leisure 15 (GR: SY494942).

THE WALK

1 With the front of the Loders Arms on your right, walk down the village street. After about 150 yards, opposite the school, the road divides.

2 Take the left-hand lane, Smishop's Lane. Sunk deep beneath tree roots, the lane runs a little uphill. Pass the lane to West Milton on the left and continue following the sign for Nettlecombe and Powerstock. The lane runs downhill and begins to curves left.

3 Just before the curve, turn right following the sign 'Public Route to Public Path'. Continue past a sign for Peascombe Nature Reserve on the right. The reserve is known for its profusion of woodland flowers and the dormice which nest in the hedgerows. The path runs to the left of the former railway embankment. Ignore a path leading up to the top of the embankment and keep straight ahead to go through a gate. Bear left for a few yards to a grassy path then bear right to continue uphill under a line of pylons with a hedge then a fence on your left.

4 At this point the path curves right downhill. **Do not follow it!** Keep straight ahead and go through a small wooden gate. Cross a farm track and take the narrow path ahead leading through the tall grass to the edge of a field. Follow the edge of the field with trees on your right as it curves left then right. Continue with trees either side of the path then a hedge on your left and go through a gate to join a wide track

LODERS – *The Loders Arms*

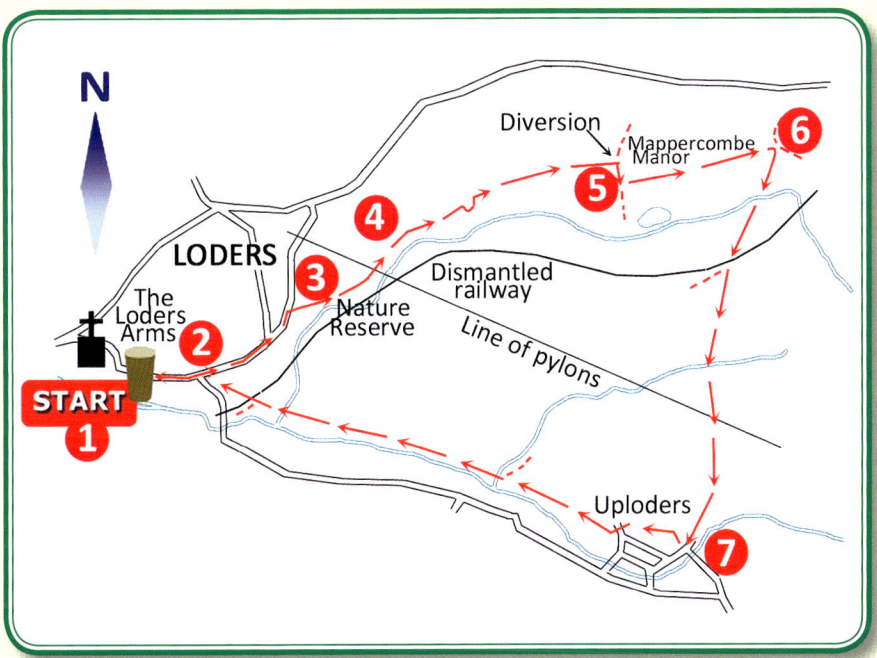

leading towards Mappercombe Manor. The manor was rebuilt in the 17th century but retains some 15th-century features.

5. The path past the manor has been diverted to avoid the buildings. As you approach the track leading left to pass the manor, turn right downhill to go through a large iron gate. (There are faint white direction signs by the gate.) Walk down the field ahead for only about 150 yards then turn left aiming for the corner of a hedge. With the hedge on your left, aim for a wooden gate. Go through the gate and continue through another gate with a hedge on your left. After going through the next gate, follow the edge of a field with hedges on the right to a cross-track.

6. Turn right down a grassy path between hedges. The path comes into the open and leads across a field. Keep straight on over a track (the former railway) and continue ahead to go under pylons towards some farm buildings.

Pub Walks in Dorset

Mappercombe Manor dates from medieval times

7 Just before the buildings, opposite a lane on the left, turn right up the tarmac track. Bear left with the buildings on your left and after about 100 yards bear slightly right along a wide green path crossing a field. After about 300 yards take the first path on the left and go through a gate. Bear right along a wide grassy track. After about 80 yards the track divides. Follow the left hand narrow path with a hedge on your left and go through a gate to take the tree-shaded riverside path. This runs to meet a lane which leads you past the old Mill, its wheel still turning, and under the railway bridge to meet the road in Loders. Turn right to walk back to the inn.

PLACE OF INTEREST NEARBY

Mangerton Mill is just north of Loders. All the mill machinery is intact and there is an agricultural museum. Open Easter week, then May to September, from 2pm to 5.30pm. (Closed Mondays.) Teas. ∅ 01308 485224; postcode DT6 3SG.

Stoke Abbot
The New Inn
4½ miles (7.2 km)

Stoke Abbott is Dorset at its most enchanting and most remote. The golden-stone houses seem lost among orchards and copse woods. Waddon Hill, rising north of the village, is crowned with the embankments of a fort built by the Romans in AD 43. Close by, the rounded crest of Gerrard's Hill provides one of the county's finest viewpoints.

Starting from the New Inn, the route of this walk takes you through woodland to follow the Wessex Ridgeway as it climbs Gerrard's Hill to the viewpoint. A terraced path then leads you over Waddon Hill past the embankments of the fort. You leave the Ridgeway to return to the village down an intriguing hollow-way. This walk in the hills is more demanding than the other walks in the book but I think the beauty of the countryside and spectacular views make the effort well worthwhile. Promise yourself a visit to Stoke Abbott's excellent New Inn as a reward!

Pub Walks in Dorset

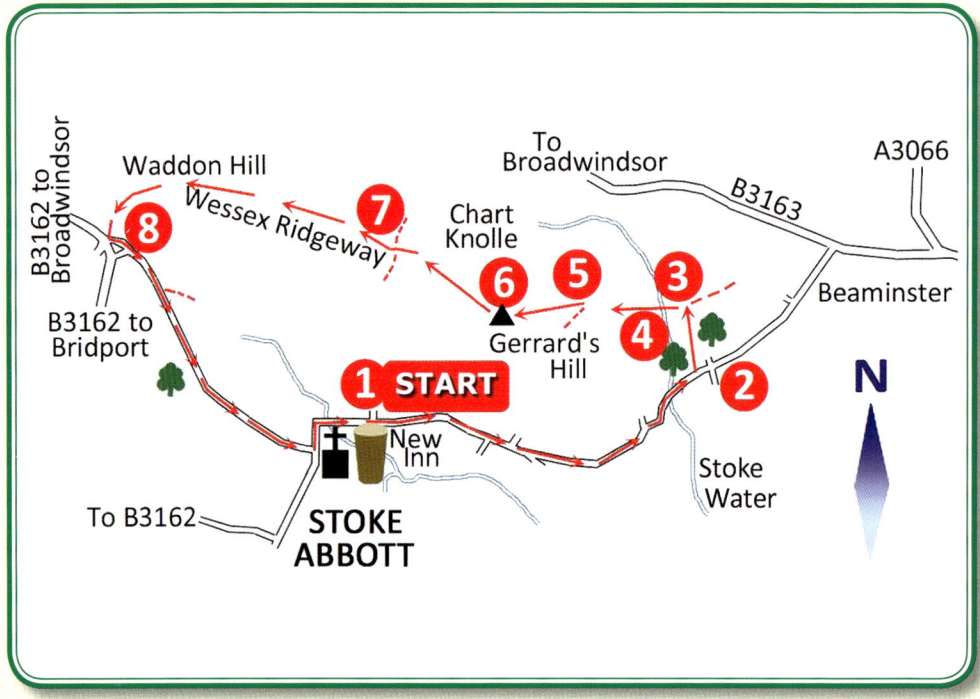

Once you have visited the hospitable 17th-century thatched **NEW INN** and enjoyed its delicious food and fine ales you will want to return. Real ales are Palmers Copper, IPA and 200. A wide range of bar snacks is available and a small but appealing menu. In winter enjoy the William Morris inspired dining area and in summer there is a beer garden where you can soak up the sunshine. The pub is popular so make sure you book ahead.
✆ 01308 868333; postcode DT8 3JW

How to get there: Stoke Abbott is about 6 miles north of Bridport. Approach via the B3162, the Bridport–Broadwindsor road. Turn for the village and continue for about ¾ mile to the village street. Turn left, follow the street round to the right and the New Inn is on your right.
Parking: In the New Inn car park.
Map: OS Explorer 29 Lyme Regis and Bridport (GR: ST453007).

Stoke Abbott – *The New Inn*

19

THE WALK

1. Turn right from the New Inn car park and continue along the lane for about ¾ mile. The lane runs beside the lower slopes of Gerrard's Hill then descends into the Stoke Water valley. Follow the lane uphill for about 200 yards to a footpath sign on the left pointing into woodland.

2. Turn left along the grassy path into the wood. Go through a gate with a Woodland Trust notice-board and follow the path through the trees to a cross-path to join the Wessex Ridgeway.

3. The route along the Ridgeway has elegantly carved signposts. Turn left following the sign for Chart Knolle. The path leads slightly downhill out of the wood and over Stoke Water to the foot of Gerrard's Hill.

4. Ignore the more obvious path leading straight ahead and bear a little right in the direction indicated by the yellow arrow footpath signs and cross a stile. Climb the steep hillside ahead to cross another stile. Continue to climb to cross the next stile almost at the top of the hill. Look back for a wonderful view of Beaminster cradled in the Brit valley.
   From the stile bear a little right over the field ahead.

5. Cross a stile, go straight over a track and through a small gate. Keep ahead then walk over to the trig point on your left to enjoy the stunning view from the top of Gerrard's Hill.

THE FOOTPATH TO GERRARD'S HILL

Pub Walks in Dorset

All Dorset seems spread at your feet. Looking east the Brit valley leads south past Bridport to West Bay. Far over the Marshwood Vale the sea glints in a dip in the coastal hills. Looking west beyond Waddon Hill rise the tree-covered slopes of Lewesdon Hill and the loaf-shaped summit of Pilsdon Pen.

6 Leaving the trig point and a group of beech trees on your left, follow the path downhill past a gate. Keep ahead with a fence and hedge on your right. Chart Knolle farmhouse is in a hollow on your left. Go through a gate and cross the grass to go over a stile. A narrow path leads steeply down through some bushes past a squeeze stile to a path.

7 Bear left along the path which descends then rises to meet a terraced path along the side of Waddon Hill. Turn right signed for Stoke Knapp. Go through a gate and follow the path along the hillside, with trees on your right and the embankments of the fort on your left. Continue ahead through the left-hand gate of the two gates you come to and walk uphill to go through a gate. Keep ahead through another gate and now it is all downhill. Walk down the wide cart track to pass some derelict farm buildings to the Broadwindsor road.

8 Here you leave the Wessex Ridgeway. Turn left and take the lane signed for Stoke Abbott. The lane is an old hollow-way plunging steeply downhill between high banks interlaced with a network of tree roots and hung with ferns. The lane meets Stoke Abbott village street. On the corner is an oak tree planted in 1901 to commemorate the accession of King Edward VII and nearby you will see two springs. One runs into a wide stone trough for animals and the other gushes out of a lion's head and is fitted with a metal cup. Turn left then follow the street round to the right to return to the New Inn.

PLACE OF INTEREST NEARBY

Redlands Yard is 2 miles north of Stoke Abbott and is a splendid place to find special gifts. You can visit the individual craft studios and watch the artists at work. There is an excellent restaurant.
✆ 01308 868362; postcode DT8 3PX

Eype
Eype's Mouth Country Hotel
2½ miles (4 km)

This is a magnificent coastal walk in the National Trust's Golden Cap Estate. From the high downs and cliff-top path you enjoy panoramic views over Lyme Bay to Portland in the east and the undulating coastline of Devon in the west. Looking inland, Bridport lies in the valley of the River Brit in the shadow of Eggardon Hill.

The walk starts at the Eype's Mouth Country Hotel in Eype, a tiny village of stone-built cottages perched either side of a narrow lane which descends a steep ravine to the beach at Eype's Mouth. Downland paths lead from the village street gradually uphill to reach the highest point of the walk at Thorncombe Beacon, 508 ft above sea level. A stroll along the South West Coast Path brings you to Eype's Mouth where you can bathe, hunt for fossils or explore the rock pools before returning to the inn.

Pub Walks in Dorset

There is a good range of menu choice at **EYPE'S MOUTH COUNTRY HOTEL**. The Smugglers Bar is open for non hotel residents where sandwiches and small plates are available along with a selection of pub favourites and delicious desserts. Traditional real ales are from local Palmers Brewery and there is a good range of wines and soft drinks. Set in a beautiful location of rolling hills and with a sea view overlooking Lyme Bay, you are likely to want to extend your stay here.
✆ 01308 423300; postcode DT6 6AL

How to get there: Eype is about ½ mile south of the A35 Bridport bypass. Leave the A35 following the sign for Eype. Pass the café and picnic area and turn left signed 'Eype's Mouth'. After a few yards, turn right signed 'Eype's Mouth'. When the road divides, take the right-hand road running downhill to the hotel which is on your right.
Parking: In Eype's Mouth Country Hotel car park.
Map: OS Explorer 29 Lyme Regis and Bridport
(GR: SY448914).

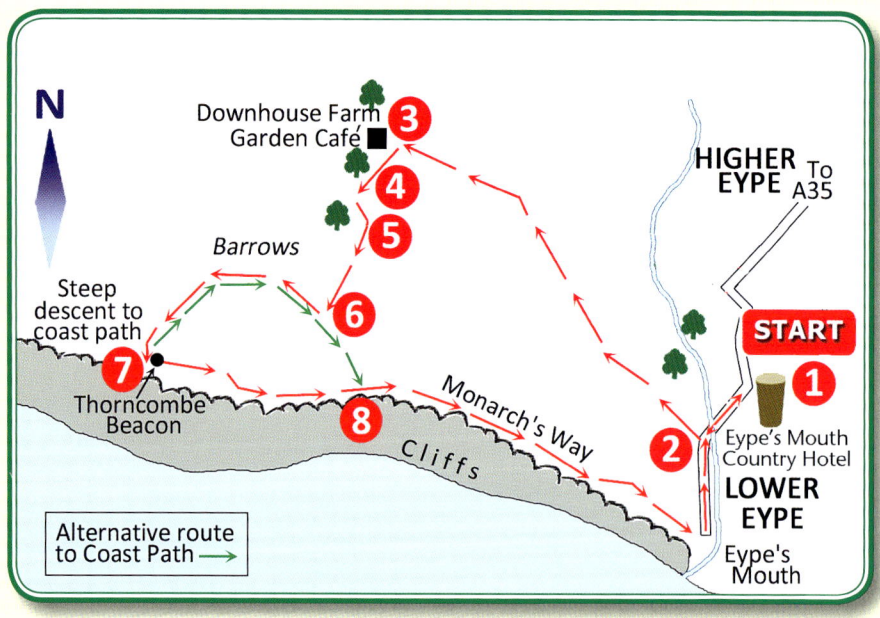

EYPE – *Eype's Mouth Country Hotel*

20

THE WALK

1. Turn right out of the hotel's car park and head downhill along the narrow lane. Just before the lane curves left and starts heading uphill, turn right along a wide gravel track marked with a National Trust sign and a sign for Eype Down.

2. Follow the track which shortly becomes grassed over. Cross a stile and bear a little right following the sign for Downhouse Farm Garden Café. Follow the downland path uphill and go through a gate signed for Eype Down. Keep ahead through a gate following the direction of the bridleway sign. Ahead you will see Down House and Downhouse Farm against a background of dense woodland. Continue through a gap in a hedge then follow the path as it swings a little left up the meadow towards the farm. Cross a stile to the lane in front of the buildings.

THE COAST PATH TO THORNCOMBE BEACON

3. Turn left and almost immediately you will see a narrow entrance on your right leading to Downhouse Farm Garden Café, the perfect refuelling stop after your climb! Continue past the café to the point where several paths meet.

4. Take the left fork signed for Little Down House. The track runs downhill then rises a little.

5. Turn left through a gate following the blue arrow bridleway sign to walk up the rise ahead. The path curves round to the right through a gate. Keep straight on with a fence on your left to a signpost.

6. At the signpost turn right signed for Eype Down and Seatown. Continue uphill to pick up a clear path rising up the down ahead. On your right you pass a large Bronze Age burial mound. The path curves left round a bowl in the down to lead you up steps to the top of Thorncombe Beacon.

The beacon is one of the chain of early warning signals erected along the South Coast where fires could be lit to warn London of impending danger. Fires burned brightly here when the Spanish Armada was sighted off Plymouth Sound. The beacon was restored in 1989 to mark the 400th anniversary of that event.

7. You have a choice of routes at this point. A very steep path leads left from Thorncombe Beacon down to meet the South West Coast Path where you can turn left to return to Eype. Or, for an easier option, retrace your steps round the bowl in the down to the signpost at point 6. This time keep straight on downhill following the sign for Eype to join the South West Coast Path.

8. Turn left to follow the coast path. Ahead, you will see the mole of Bridport's tiny harbour, West Bay, sandwiched between sheer sandstone cliffs and, beyond, the low arc of the Chesil beach. After about a mile the path descends to the beach at Eype's Mouth. Turn left to walk up the narrow lane until you reach Eype's Mouth Country Hotel on your left.

PLACE OF INTEREST NEARBY

Charmouth Heritage Centre is west of Eype near Lyme Regis. Here you can discover more about the history and geology of the Jurassic Coast. There is a wide range of colourful displays and interactive computers that enable you to take a virtual dive beneath the waters of Lyme Bay and to identify the fossils you may find on the beaches. Entrance is free. Opening times vary. ✆ 01297 560772; postcode DT6 6LL